Sleeping Giant Publishing, LLC
www.sleepinggiantpublishing.com

PHD Dissertation

The University of Arizona/Department of Philosophy
Stephen J. Lenhart, PhD

Cognitive Diversity and the Progress of Science

A Dissertation Submitted to the Faculty of the
Department of Philosophy
In Partial Fulfillment of the Requirements
For the Degree of
Doctor of Philosophy
In the Graduate College
The University of Arizona

19 April 2011

Copyright © 2011 by Stephen J. Lenhart

All rights reserved, including the right to reproduce this work or portions thereof in any form whatsoever.
For more information address Sleeping Giant Publishing at www.sleepinggiantpublishing.com

Manufactured and printed in the United States of America

ISBN: 978-0-9835277-4-9
Library of Congress Cataloging-in-Publication Data

COGNITIVE DIVERSITY AND THE PROGRESS OF SCIENCE

by

Stephen J. Lenhart

A Dissertation Submitted to the Faculty of the

DEPARTMENT OF PHILOSOPHY

In Partial Fulfillment of the Requirements
For the Degree of

DOCTOR OF PHILOSOPHY

In the Graduate College

THE UNIVERSITY OF ARIZONA

2 0 1 1

THE UNIVERSITY OF ARIZONA
GRADUATE COLLEGE

As members of the Dissertation Committee, we certify that we have read the dissertation

prepared by Stephen J. Lenhart

entitled Cognitive Diversity and The Progress of Science

and recommend that it be accepted as fulfilling the dissertation requirement for the

Degree of Doctor of Philosophy

_____ Date: 19 April 2011
Richard Healey

_____ Date: 19 April 2001
Jenann Ismael

_____ Date: 19 April 2011
Shaughan Lavine

_____ Date:

_____ Date:

Final approval and acceptance of this dissertation is contingent upon the candidate's submission of the final copies of the dissertation to the Graduate College.

I hereby certify that I have read this dissertation prepared under my direction and recommend that it be accepted as fulfilling the dissertation requirement.

_____ Date: 19 April 2011
Dissertation Director: Richard Healey

STATEMENT BY AUTHOR

This dissertation has been submitted in partial fulfillment of requirements for an advanced degree at The University of Arizona and is deposited in the University Library to be made available to borrowers under rules of the Library.

Brief quotations from this dissertation are allowable without special permission, provided that accurate acknowledgment of source is made. Requests for permission for extended quotation from or reproduction of this manuscript in whole or in part may be granted by the head of the major department or the Dean of the Graduate College when in his or her judgment the proposed use of the material is in the interests of scholarship. In all other instances, however, permission must be obtained from the author.

SIGNED: _____ STEPHEN J. LENHART

ACKNOWLEDGMENTS

This dissertation has benefited from many philosophical interactions, some of which occurred before this dissertation was even a collection of fragmentary thoughts. Those exchanges often ranged far outside the topics of this dissertation, but in the spirit of the present thesis about cognitive diversity, I wish to recognize the value of doing philosophy with Anne Baril, Matt Bedke, Jacob Caton, Tom Christiano, Helen Daly, Jake Daly, Patrick Dieveney, Don Falis, Justin Fisher, Michael Gil, David Glick, Alan Habib, Michelle Jenkins, Marc Johansen, Rachana Kamtekar, Keith Lehrer, Bill Lycan, Kay Mathiesen, Jason Matteson, David Owen, John Pollock, John T. Roberts, Dave Schmidtz, Paul Thorn, Justin Tosi, Kevin Vallier, and Sarah Wright.

Among my interlocutors, my dissertation committee deserves separate acknowledgment. Thanks to Jenann Ismael and Shaughan Lavine for their criticisms, suggestions, and insights. My director, Richard Healey, deserves special recognition for his patience, advice, and assistance in nearly every aspect of this work.

The support of good friends has been invaluable, and I thank them all for their support. Three deserve special mention, as we endured writing our dissertations together: Helen Daly, Michelle Jenkins, and Marc Johansen. For thrity-two years of loving support, I also thank my mother, Elona Lenhart.

Finally, I wish to thank my wife Laura. She is a mentor, a friend, and a philosopher without whom this would not have been possible.

Table of Contents

LIST OF FIGURES 7

ABSTRACT 8

CHAPTER 1. PROGRESS 10
   1.1. Science 13
   1.2. Progress 20
   1.3. Accuracy 24
      1.3.1. Models and Accuracy 30
      1.3.2. Objections from Fundamental Physics 35
   1.4. The Project 37

CHAPTER 2. JUSTIFYING AGREEMENT 39
   2.1. Diversity and Convergence 39
   2.2. Geological Science and Scientific Development 48
   2.3. Scientific Progress and the Merits of Diversity 62
      2.3.1. Computational Results Favoring Diversity 63
      2.3.2. Inseparability of Discovery and Certification 74

CHAPTER 3. EXPLAINING PROGRESS 80
   3.1. The Explanatory Defense of Progress 81
   3.2. Pessimistic Objections 87
   3.3. Pessimism and Realism 89
   3.4. Brief Histories: Oxygen and Caloric 95
   3.5. Lessons from History 100

CHAPTER 4. THE AIMS OF SCIENCE OR LACK THEREOF 108
   4.1. Does Science Have Aims? 111
      4.1.1. Reductionism 112
      4.1.2. Explanations of norms 121
      4.1.3. Vague Aims 126
      4.1.4. Brute Facts? 129
      4.1.5. The Standard Realist Aim 130
   4.2. Reconsidering Aims of Science 133

CHAPTER 5. KNOWLEDGE AND SCIENTIFIC DEVELOPMENT 135
   5.1. The Aim of Belief 137
   5.2. Knowledge and Scientific Development 142

TABLE OF CONTENTS—*Continued*

5.3. Knowledge and Progress 152

REFERENCES **157**

LIST OF FIGURES

FIGURE 1.1.	The Simple Harmonic Oscillator	31
FIGURE 2.1.	The consensus model of scientific development	42
FIGURE 2.2.	The convergence model of scientific development	43
FIGURE 3.1.	Convergence and the Explanatory Defense	85
FIGURE 5.1.	Bird's Thought Experiment	153

Abstract

Science benefits from substantial cognitive diversity because cognitive diversity promotes scientific progress toward greater accuracy. Without diversity of goals, beliefs, and methods, science would neither generate novel discoveries nor certify representations with its present effectiveness. The revolution in geosciences is a principal case study.

The role of cognitive diversity in discovery is explored with attention to computational results. Discovery and certification are inseparable. Moreover, diverse scientific groups agree convergently, and their agreements manifest an explanatory defense akin to the explanatory defense of realism. Scientists accept representations as a matter of their instrumental success in individual scientific research. Because scientists are diverse, this standard of acceptance means that widespread acceptance involves widespread instrumental success. This success is best explained through the accuracy of topics of agreement.

The pessimistic induction is addressed; it fails to undermine the explanatory defense because past scientific successes don't resemble present ones in their degree of instrumental success; to make this point, instrumental success of representations of caloric and of oxygen are compared.

Cognitive diversity challenges the methodological uniformity of scientific practice. Science lacks uniform methods and aims, and it ought to. It is argued that there is no sound basis for thinking that science aims. Moreover, the growth of science itself is not the growth of knowledge. Scientific communities rather than individual scientists are the main certifiers of scientific results. Hence, since knowledge requires a certifying belief formation process but the process relevant to science is not realized individually, science does not progress toward knowledge. The epistemology of science is socialized, but remains broadly realist because, even without a method of inquiry, science develops accurate representations of unobservable nature.

CHAPTER 1

PROGRESS

This dissertation addresses the subjects of progress, rationality, and knowledge within science. Those issues are traditional ones in the philosophy of science, and lie at the heart of the debate among scientific realists, empiricists, and social constructivists. These three positions are genuses, not species, and no brief discussion could catalog the various ways that they have been realized. Nevertheless, it is helpful to contrast these three positions in their assessment of the processes and achievements they attribute to science. Realists and empiricists agree with one another, and oppose social constructivists, in believing that science obtains objective representations of a mind-independent world. Furthermore, realists and empiricists agree that science is epistemically privileged in the sense that alternative means of producing representations of a mind-independent world are less successful than science is. Traditionally, realists and empiricists have attributed this epistemic privilege to the possession of rational methods of inquiry, and herein lies the source of their disagreement with social constructivists.[1]

Social constructivists resist this rationalist bent of realism and empiricism; they allege that the principle sources of scientific influence are social forces that scientists create. Realists and empiricists, by contrast, allege that scientific methods involve interactions with nature that overcome social forces: ultimately, according to these rationalist views, scientific judgments are constrained by nature and the representations that science produces thereby accurately represent it. Social constructivists also

---

[1] In the present chapter, rationalism is just the thesis that individually manifest rational methods of inquiry rule the day in science; the thesis is deliberately vague within the sketch of realism, empiricism and constructivism that this chapter offers. In chapter 2, I discuss a more precise characterization of rationalism due to Phillip Kitcher; I argue that, despite his disavowals, Kitcher retains a key component of rationalism that we should abandon.

deny the epistemic privilege of science. Scientific agreements are the results of social forces that are in no special respect different from the social forces that ruled indigenous communities of America, for example; consequently, while rationalists have held that science gets special consideration as a means to advancing inquiry and as an arbiter of debates about nature, constructivists reject these claims.

The source of this disagreement about rationalism lies in differential assessments of the operative forces in scientific communities; particular attention has been paid to disagreement. No party to the discussion can deny that scientists sometimes disagree, though that fact alone cannot tell for or against rationalism. The merits of rationalists's account of scientific development are exposed in the sources of disagreement and its resolution. If disagreements are eliminated by processes for which we can claim epistemic privilege, the reliability of science is sustained. The burden for rationalists is thus two-fold: identify the processes that rule the day in scientific inquiry and demonstrate that those processes are epistemically privileged.

Rationalists, of course, find themselves in significant disagreement over the extent of scientific achievements. Empiricists contend that the limit of scientific achievement involves what's empirically accessible. The exact nature of empirical accessibility is the subject of much debate, but clearly outside its scope are objects too small to be detected by human sense organs, natural kinds, and real (nomic) dependence relations. Realists likewise debate the limits of scientific achievement, though all agree that some of what's empirically inaccessible is within the scope of scientific achievement. Realists also disagree with one another about the epistemic ground for claims about the empirically inaccessible. Nevertheless, realists typically advance some claim to the effect that description of unobservables would have little empirical success unless there were some truth to the descriptions of unobservables.

The history of science presents challenges to realists' commitments regarding unobservables. Because the history of science involves many changes in its ontological picture of unobservable entities, empiricists naturally point to greater stability of experimental and observational facts as evidence for empiricism and against realism. Realists often point out that theories of unobservables improve the precision of our descriptions of empirical regularities, but this fact alone will not save realism from the naïve version that erroneously alleges ontological continuity in the sciences. Realists thus typically claim that science *progresses* so that it improves the accuracy of the description of the world that it provides.

The view presented in this dissertation most closely matches scientific realism. I argue that science progresses toward greater accuracy, and I don't play favorites with observables. My reasons for thinking that science progresses are cousins of realist reasons, but I reject the methodological commitment of rationalism, which seeks to locate the epistemic privilege of science within the possession of a method of inquiry. However, rationalists' burden to identify the processes that rule the day in scientific inquiry and demonstrate that those processes are epistemically privileged can nevertheless be discharged by locating these processes within the scientific community, rather than scientific individuals, processes that secure the reliability of the community and the accuracy of its representations.

Emphasis on scientific communities is not new, and the heuristic picture of realists and their opponents above does little justice to the degree to which, in recent decades, realists have attended to social factors within science. However, rationalist philosophies of science have typically hoped to recover rational methods from social constructivist criticism. This dissertation eschews rational (individual) methods in favor of processes that are communally manifest, and I argue that these processes are the ones that realize scientific progress toward accuracy.

In addition to being about these particular subjects, this is also a dissertation about science and cognitive diversity. A recurring theme in discussions related to these topics is that cognitive diversity forces a philosophical reassessment of science. Cognitive diversity is a force behind discovery and certification of scientific results; science without cognitive diversity would be a less potent instrument for exploring and understanding nature: cognitive diversity promotes progress. Cognitive diversity manifests as disagreement, not only about scientific representations, but about goals and practices of scientists. Whereas social constructivists have typically regarded such disagreement as evidence of irrationality in science and often claimed that it undercuts rationalist claims to the epistemic privilege of science, I claim that such diversity is a substantial element of having that epistemic privilege. A point of convergence between anti-rationalist and rationalist accounts of science has been that the epistemic privilege of science rests on individually manifest rationality: my account eschews rationality in the explanatory story of scientific development (with anti-rationalists) but locates elements in the social process of agreement formation that underwrite the epistemic privilege of science.

The next few sections (§1.1–1.3) of this chapter explain the claim that science progresses toward greater accuracy; the final section (§1.4) outlines the rest of this dissertation.

1.1 Science

"Science" is an ambiguous term. Scholars of science, lay persons, and scientists themselves all use it. Scholars of science include historians, sociologists, philosophers and scientists themselves. Consequently, what exactly tokens of 'science' denote, if they denote anything *exactly*, is an open question. Context or the stipulations of an author settle the question if anything does. 'Science' has sometimes been associated with the pattern of behavior by which humans gain control over their environment; science in this sense includes the development of metal working, agriculture, navigation and calendar creation as well as the more abstract bodies of thought associated with those developments. A narrower conception of science distinguishes theoretical belief from its applications; metal working, agriculture and so forth are thus conceived as technologies distinct from the theoretical beliefs associated with their development.

But not merely any body of theoretical belief would count as science. According to some, it is those theoretical beliefs about nature, which in their origin are theoretical beliefs that allow us to gain control over our environment, that count as science.[2] According to others, it is beliefs formed in accordance with certain (typically empirical) methodological principles, perhaps also involving beliefs of a general, law-like, or explanatory character. 'Science' is sometimes associated more loosely with a character of objectivity and willingness to confront empirical refutation: Sherlock Holmes' approach to crimes is, in this sense, scientific.[3]

Within this dissertation, the usual contrasts with 'science' and 'scientific' are 'non-science' and 'non-scientific', not 'pseudoscience' and 'unscientific'. Of art, politics, or baking, the term 'unscientific' is misplaced because the term applies criteria of assessment inappropriate to the topic. On the other hand, astrology and creationism are typically thought to be unscientific. Roughly speaking, what's unscientific is something that lacks epistemic privilege while pretending to be part of real science. But astrology and creationism are also non-science in the sense of the present work; what's non-science (roughly speaking) is what is not a part or product of the community of scientists. Neither creationism nor astrology has any (present) acceptance within the our community of scientists. When clarity is important, I shall say 'descriptively scientific' and 'evaluatively scientific' to mark the contrast respectively with non-scientific and unscientific. A substantial goal of this dissertation is to show that descriptively scientific stuff is evaluatively scientific.

For the purposes of understanding scientific progress, we must be open to the realities of history. If, for example, we claim that science is characterized by a certain empirical methodology, we run the risk of (accidentally) supposing that science was invented in the middle of the 19th century. Additionally, methodological character-

---

[2]David Lindberg [Lin92, 2] notes that in the middle ages, the latin *scientia* included theology and metaphysics as well as natural philosophy. Interesting historical notes aside, I don't include metaphysics or theology in the extension of 'science.'

[3]The present, incomplete catalog of uses of 'science' is adapted from Lindberg [Lin92].

izations of science occasionally blind scholars to causes of scientific change because the causes were "unscientific." Similar problems arise if we identify science with a particular body of theoretical beliefs, or even more broadly with theoretical belief and its applications. To avoid these problems, I propose that science be characterized historically and sociologically. Science in a given era is the practice and product of that era's community of scientists; past communities of scientists are identified with the communities that are historical antecedents of present scientific communities.[4]

If we reach back far enough, we will have to ask whether very old antecedents of scientific communities, such as alchemists, were scientists in their day. These questions are subtle. Alchemists (for example) did investigate nature, and the burden of proof rests with those who wish to claim that alchemists were largely unsystematic and irrational investigators of nature.[5] In these respects, alchemists are similar to modern scientists. However, there are differences as well, such as the largely secretive nature of the practice, and in evaluative respects alchemists may seem unscientific by present standards. Nevertheless, alchemy did not (like modern astrology) fly in the face of established epistemic authority, nor is it clear that alchemists weren't doing their epistemic best, given the limited knowledge of nature they possessed.[6] In light of these considerations, though alchemical practice would not today be scientific (in either sense), I maintain that alchemists were scientists in their day. More generally speaking, where we draw the line between societies of cave men and modern physicists (the former are antecedents of the latter) will be in some respects arbitrary; communities on the modern side of this boundary are progressive.

Science in the present day is an institution with fairly clear sociological bound-

---

[4] Kuhn [Kuh70] discusses a similar means of understanding "scientific" in section one of the postscript. I disagree with his characterization of these groups as ideologically homogeneous, but his criteria of sociological individuation are similar.

[5] In a BBC documentary on the Middle Ages, it was reported that alchemists' quest to make gold from other substances was motivated in part by the fact that gold is "incorruptible."

[6] The considerations of chapter 2 may suggest that *their* epistemic best was better for them than our best would have been, given their limited knowledge of nature. However, I will not take up this claim specifically regarding alchemy.

aries. Without reference to subject matter or methods, scientific groups are readily identified by their members' affiliation with academic institutions and professional organizations. The boundaries thus defined, especially when we consider professional organizations, reveal that science is a multi-layered community. Academic departments divide the scientific community only in the coarsest way, leaving us with biology, physics, chemistry, geoscience and others as natural sciences, with psychology, economics, sociology, linguistics, medicine, and others as human sciences. Professional associations and journals demarcate these groups further and may indicate overlaps in some sub-disciplines of sciences. More specialized groups are indicated by somewhat less formal sociological features, such as attending special conferences, lying in a network of communication regarding certain results and studies before their publication and completion, and occurring in patterns of citation in published pieces. [Kuh70, 177–78]

Because science is multi-layered, it is reasonable to ask what exactly progresses? My answer is that science as a whole progresses, but does so because individual sciences do. Individual sciences are those broad fields typically identified with academic departments. Some sub-fields of individual sciences progress, but here things become more complex; the boundaries among sub-fields of sciences are more plastic than the boundaries at the highest levels. Consequently, sub-fields of sciences are born and die, and move from the periphery to the center (and vice-versa) as scientific specializations. Sometimes, in one variety of scientific unification, sub-fields are absorbed into other sub-fields.[7]

Something should strike the reader at this point: what are the products of a

---

[7]Changes in the program of education in physics illustrate this plasticity. Fifty years ago, the core courses of a physics education included mechanics, electricity and magnetism, optics and thermodynamics, and many programs today still follow this model. The Massachusetts Institute of Technology does not: today their recommended path for a degree as preparation for study in graduate level physics includes one course each in statistical physics, relativity, experimental physics and multiple courses in quantum mechanics. This clearly reflects the degree to which physics today is quantum physics and other fields that developed since the early twentieth century.

community that we assess for accuracy? The answer varies according to the particular claim about progress that we are assessing; in the present case, the answer is representations about which the scientific community has achieved agreement.[8] (I shall have a considerable amount to say about representations in section 1.3 below; for the moment I ask my reader to bear with me as I discuss representations while saying little about what these are.) The representational content of a science at a time lies in the representations that nearly all the members of that community accept. Agreement occurs when scientists for the most part uniformly accept that some representation is accurate, perhaps for specified purposes or within a restricted range. For our purposes, acceptance is a matter of scientists' dispositions to accept a representation as accurate, rather than explicitly doing so. Many of the representations that scientists produce never receive explicit acceptance at the community level because too few members of the community are aware of the representations. Despite not having explicit acceptance, these representations may enjoy implicit acceptance if the members of a community are disposed to explicitly accept them without exceptional scrutiny. The condition *without exceptional scrutiny* is meant to eliminate those representations that would require more than acquaintance and casual inspection in order to be accepted. The reason to countenance acceptance in this dispositional way is that a wide range of scientific work builds in a straightforward and uncontroversial way upon established science (it is "normal" in Kuhn's sense) and needs little to be accepted within the scientific community. Obviously the volume of such "normal" scientific work extends beyond any individual's capacity for explicit acceptance; a dispositional account remedies this defect.

The dispositions of scientists to accept representations from other fields will tend to track the degree to which members of that field have agreed; ordinarily, scientists regard members of other scientific fields as experts to defer to in most matters

---

[8]In section 1.2 I offer pluralism about targets of progress; the topic of this dissertation is but one form of progress about which to inquire.

regarding their own field. This is not always the case, however. Kelvin famously complained about the age of the earth according to Darwinian biology and its associated geoscience. An exciting modern example involves theories of the origin of life: "replicator first" and "metabolism first" are schools of thought in the search for these theories; the metabolism first view finds its prominent adherents among geoscientists, who argue that the under-sea conditions when life first evolved would have ensured the genesis of metabolic reactions including adenosine triphosphate; the biological community is much more likely to pursue replicator first theories that look to places where RNA and DNA would have first arisen.[9] Scientists within a field are less likely to defer to authority in the straightforward way that those external to the field do. Scientists are more sensitive to the work that has clear implications for their own research.[10]

Three important points are worth making at this juncture: the products of scientific activity are not exclusively representations; agreement is not necessarily desirable in scientific communities[11]; representations need not be an end state of scientific inquiry, i.e., representations about which science achieves consensus may be instrumen-

---

[9]This debate is a fascinating one about which I am still learning. My reader is advised to see the news feature in *Nature*, 21 May 2009, [Whi09].

[10]Chapter 2 offers considerable evidence on behalf of this claim, as well as argument against the authority view that says scientists mostly repeat the beliefs of authorities.

[11]Miriam Solomon [Sol01, 97–100] criticizes what she calls "the consensus about consensus" among philosophers of science. That view is, roughly, the idea scientific communities should eliminate dissent, or that it a goal of science to achieve agreement. Solomon instead aligns herself with Mill and Feyerabend, but against the rest of philosophical community, in claiming that dissent is symptomatic of health. I agree about the desirability of dissent. (I'm somewhat unsure about her diagnosis of a "consensus about consensus".) One way for science to progress is to dissolve agreement; but dissolving agreement is only positive when it is progressive, i.e., when undesirable agreement is eliminated. Regarding accuracy, an increase in dissent is good when it constitutes the rejection of an inaccurate representation. (This point becomes rather subtle because many representations are accurate only in a relative sense; see 1.3 below.) In my view, changes in agreement are progressive or regressive; neither agreement nor disagreement has any intrinsic value.

My valuations, however, look to the changes in agreement. That is because I know of nothing else to identify with the practice and product of the scientific community, i.e., the science. Changes to the community might promote or hinder progress, but those changes are not changes in the science and hence, seem not to count as progress or regress—that they are sometimes thus identified seems to me whigish, *post hoc* evaluation.

tal to achieving some other task, and that task may or may not be representational.

Anti-representationalists have sometimes taken thoughts similar to these too far in the opposite extreme, claiming, for example, that scientists don't make judgments of accuracy of the sort required on my view at all.[12] But the claim that science does not aim at representation (or that scientists do not so aim) is nevertheless compatible with the view that scientists make such judgments: Scientists' presentation of their own work often frames it as an attempt to answer a question, and their answers are descriptive claims about nature (or a relationship between nature and a model), not practical advice or instructions. Objections from one scientist to another often take the form of claiming that a particular representation is inaccurate, or accurate only under limited conditions, or accurate only given a certain tolerance for error. The widespread practice of describing an assumption as "simplifying" is often best understood as acknowledging and accepting a level of inaccuracy while contending that the representation (and perhaps its inaccuracy) is useful.[13] Scientists may judge a measurement technique as more accurate than another, an assessment that presumably involves comparison of representations that result from measurement.[14] Examination of the practice of science sometimes reveals no appreciation for accuracy, but overt discussion of scientific results reveals assessments of representational accuracy, even if these *assessments* are not *appreciations*. The modest version of anti-representationalism, which denies that science aims to represent, is compatible with accepting that scientists nevertheless judge accuracy, and this latter view better comports with many attitudes of scientists toward their work and that of others.[15]

---

[12] Jenann Ismael has in conversation pressed me to respond to an objection to my characterization of science along these lines.

[13] I'm grateful to Shaughan Lavine who pointed out that I oversimplified this situation in a previous draft: simplifying assumptions usually reveal a scientist's preference for something acquired in exchange for accuracy, not simple tolerance of inaccuracy. The main point here is not whether and what scientists exchange accuracy for but that scientists make assessments of accuracy even if accuracy is not their goal.

[14] Richard Healey drew my attention to this particular sort of assessment in what I take to have been a complimentary point.

[15] I give further discussion of scientific representation itself and accuracy of these representations

1.2 Progress

Whether science progresses is a question about how science changes. Some changes in science are improvements, some changes unimportant, some deteriorations. A theory of scientific progress tells us which changes are which. A theory of scientific progress also tells us more than that, for science is not progressive if improvements at one time are canceled by subsequent deteriorations at another. Hence, a theory of progress tells us which improvements science typically exhibits. Improvements mean getting better, and an important distinction among good things bears on the matter of scientific progress: some things are good because they allow us to achieve other good things while other things are good in themselves.[16] Among the products and practices of science are practices for allocating resources, for educating students, and for crediting success. While these have important ramifications for the products and practices of science, they are not themselves good or bad, but only good or bad insofar as they conduce to other things.[17] It would be unusual to say that improvements in funding practices were progress; rather, those improvements promote progress. Progress occurs with improvements valuable for their own sake.

Thus, science progresses toward x if and only if (1) science for the most part monotonically improves in relation to x, and (2) x is not merely instrumentally valuable. This allows that science might improve as a means to reducing human suffering, by

---

in 1.3 below. It will emerge, for example, that the notion of accuracy is often relative rather than absolute, and that judgments of accuracy are consequently comparative rather than absolute. Since scientific progress is about changes (see 1.2) and increases in accuracy, relative accuracy and comparative judgment are perfectly appropriate to the present context.

[16]Of course, some things are both good instrumentally and good in themselves.

[17]Allocation of resources, methods of education and standards of citation may involve matters of justice, in which case certain changes could be good in themselves rather than simply for what they produce.

I would certainly endorse improvements of science with respect to justice, but matters of social progress lie outside the scope of this dissertation. The 20th century certainly saw progress on the front of equality of opportunity for women and racial minorities, and since the scientific revolution, science has increasingly become an occupation for the qualified rather than a hobby of the aristocracy: there is some case to be made that science progresses regarding justice as well as accuracy. A full discussion of justice and science is outside the scope of this dissertation.

increasing the accuracy of representations of nature, by enabling more efficient use of natural resources, and many other things. The first condition rules out something as a target of scientific progress if science merely occasionally or haphazardly improves regarding that thing. The second condition rules out taking science to progress simply because it regularly exhibits certain features that conduce to targets of genuine progress. For example, science more or less monotonically increases the population of scientists and this is certainly instrumentally valued because it increases the efficacy of science regarding other things valued non-instrumentally; (2) rules that out as genuine progress. In the present context, at least, I must admit that the boundary between instrumental and non-instrumental value is vague: aren't antibiotics an *instrument* for curing disease? In some sense they are, but antibiotics lie so close to the end of curing disease that the latter end is (almost) achieved by the development of the former tool. This is unlike better advertising of degrees in sciences, which, though it is very likely to improve the sciences, cannot be linked to any particular end.

The thesis of this dissertation thus amounts to claiming that science for the most part monotonically improves regarding accuracy, and that accuracy is valuable not merely instrumentally. The claim that accuracy is valuable in itself is apt to raise some eyebrows. By way of defense, let me first say that I'm offering an analysis of progress that takes value as primitive. I take the present account to be compatible with nearly any axiology. Perhaps subjectivism about value is correct, so that if we care about accuracy, that is enough to establish its value. Perhaps some rich transcendental argument can establish a contradiction in being a cognitive agent that doesn't value accuracy. But even those skeptical about the intrinsic worth of accurate representations should accept that accuracy often has a high level of instrumental worth. Furthermore, accuracy is constitutive of certain philosophical and scientific goals such as explanation: one has an explanation merely in form, but not in substance, if one's explanans is wholly inaccurate. Consequently, the thesis of this dissertation establishes an interesting claim, that science improves regarding accuracy.

My thesis should not be taken to exclude forms of progress besides progress toward accuracy. Among the targets of scientific progress, accuracy is just one. Insofar as many things are valuable in themselves, many things are potential targets of scientific progress. And so, scientific progress may be a pluralistic affair. Science builds bridges, understands markets, and prevents disease. Science is an integral part of our capacity to succeed in our endeavors.[18]

Though I doubt this particular misunderstanding will arise, I should address it here: The discourse of progress involves metaphors of motion and targets. Progress is thus sometimes conceived as motion toward a target, with the target conceived as an end state, so that upon reaching the target, motion should cease. In the context of this dissertation, one might then suppose that progress is getting ever close to the one true (accurate) description of the natural world. However, that conception is mistaken. It is no business of this work to claim that the natural world has one true description, nor that we need to conceive of such a description as an ideal in order to understand progress. Changes in science can be assessed in pairwise comparisons of temporally successive stages of science. (Kitcher shares this in his account, see [Kit93, 91].) Put less epistemically, changes in science exist as a matter of differences among successive stages. Any appearance of motion toward a goal thus emerges from relations between these stages. Indeed, with regard to accuracy, I shall argue that relative differences in accuracy may exist even if there are no facts of the matter about instantaneous states of accuracy for individual stages of science.

It is crucial to note that progress says nothing about scientific decision making, i.e., to say "x is progress" does not entail that x is or should be a consideration of scientists in their scientific decisions. What counts as an improvement to the community's agreement need not be a consideration for individual scientists working on

---

[18]Science has also been a partner in the most atrocious of human crimes. Nowhere sees the the technological progress of humanity more acutely than war. Even where we distinguish technology from science, science facilitates technological change.

their individual tasks. To put this point another way, a theory of scientific progress is not a normative theory that announces a standard of appraisal for scientists. Indeed, I shall argue in chapter 2 that scientists do not share a standard of theory appraisal, and that this is a profitable state of affairs that explains scientific progress regarding accuracy.

The notion of a progressive science sometimes includes accumulation and development with past results as a basis of current research. Such a view of science holds that it becomes successively more comprehensive, first by tackling simple problems, then by extending itself to more complex ones. Within this conception, regarding some questions, science provides permanent and fixed answers that settle the matter. Few philosophers endorse such a view today because it is falsified by history, and for that reason this dissertation does not endorse this cumulative conception of scientific progress. A related notion one might call a dialectic conception of scientific progress. According to such a view, scientific research typically incorporates and responds to the science of its day; the dialectic conception does not hold that science preserves the results of past science, but it does hold that scientific development is a kind of path dependent process that proceeds from accepted results to new ones, even when those new results replace their predecessors. In both the dialectic and cumulative views of progress, accuracy has traditionally played a role. Within the cumulative view, science progresses by establishing truths. The dialectic view, at least among scientific realists, has attempted to account for the success in scientific development by claiming that accuracy, once possessed, begets a dialectical starting point from which further development will beget more accuracy. This view has been elaborated within the explanatory defense of realism, and I discuss it in detail in chapter 3. My own account of scientific development is not cumulative but dialectical.

To summarize the view so far: Science is the practice and product of the scientific community. Included in that product are the representations about which that community has achieved consensus. Because accurate representations are valuable and science reveals consensus on successively more accurate representations, science progresses toward greater accuracy. Up to this point, I have said little about the representations that science produces, what accuracy is, or how to assess the increase in accuracy of scientific agreement; these are the issues of the next section.

1.3 Accuracy

Science uses many forms of representation to depict nature. Among these, linguistic descriptions are the most familiar, and a number of historically significant scientific representations can be expressed with words alone: hearts pump blood, the sun is the center of the heavens, calxes absorb phlogiston when heated in the presence of charcoal, yeast causes fermentation, lightning is electricity—the list goes on. These and other descriptions are accurate when true and inaccurate when false. Thus, the improvement of science with respect to the accuracy of linguistic descriptions involves increase in the number of accepted truths and decrease in the number of accepted falsehoods. With respect to linguistic representations, there are actually two potential dimensions of improvement: the increase of accuracy and the decrease of inaccuracy.

Truth and falsity, though familiar enough notions, present several puzzles on the way to saying what increasing accuracy is. For this reason, I begin my analysis focusing on them exclusively. For the duration of this section, I will occasionally speak as though scientific representations are principally linguistic. If scientific representations are principally linguistic, that's a contingent historical fact about how scientists have represented nature, not a deep truth about scientific activity.

Saying exactly what increasing overall accuracy is requires further investigation. In the most straightforward case, scientific agreement changes to include more truths and fewer falsehoods, and this is unequivocally progress toward truth. In other cases, however, science will increase both truths and falsehoods, and in others decrease both. For the limited standpoint of saying that an increase of truths is progress and that the decrease in falsehoods is progress, these latter two cases are indeterminate. The indeterminacy of the former case is especially unsettling because a great deal of scientific advancement would seem to involve increase of truth and falsehood both: most important new developments of science, especially those that engage new domains, will bring some falsehoods as well as truths.

As a heuristic, one may conceive changes in the accuracy of a collection of scientific representations by thinking about science as an advisor in making bets. Imagine that you are about to be confronted with a number of betting opportunities and have nothing but the advice of your advisor to go on. You would like to make as much money as possible. In each bet, you are offered a proposition and odds that it is true; you may bet for or against each proposition, and you may decline to bet altogether. In this game, we always make bets for a fixed sum; we can never bet more or less because we think the odds are especially good or bad. Moreover, all bets are at the same odds and those odds reflect the relative frequency of truth among the total set of bets you will be offered. Hence, if you were to give the same response to every betting opportunity, you would break even.[19]

Suppose that you don't know what bets you will be offered, what would you want from your advisor? Ideally, the advice is always correct and it covers every situation you encounter, i.e., you make a bet every time you are offered one and the bet you make is always correct. However, your advisor is not ideal in either of these respects: some bets he will suggest are going to lose and sometimes he counsels against betting. Changes in our advisor that would improve our betting circumstance model what changes to our advisor would be improvements in his accuracy. All other

---

[19]Here are what the elements of this model represent: making money represents having an accurate picture of the world; your goal of making as much as possible represents desiring a maximally accurate picture of the world. The odds don't represent much at all presently, but if we extend the picture to include significance, odds could represent significance of truths. The fixed sum of all bets represents that no particular bet is more important than any other, and hence that we are presently ignoring significance. (There are two symmetric ways to represent significance, each changes the investment in a particular bet; one is to vary the odds offered, the other is to vary the sum of the bets.) This particular model thus neglects the significance of truths.

things being equal, an increase in the number of truths is an improvement because an increase in truths is an increase in correct betting opportunities. An increase in the number of falsehoods would be acceptable when it was accompanied by an even greater increase in the number of truths accepted, for though this would increase the number of losing bets I would make, it would increase more the number of winning bets I would make.[20] A decrease in the number of truths accepted would mean fewer opportunities to make bets, but it would be acceptable if the number of bad bets I would accept were decreased.[21]

The number of correct bets one will make equals the number of times one will accept a bet times the probability, for any given bet, that the bet is winning. The number of times one bets equals the rate of having answers to the questions times the number of bets offered. Since the number of bets offered is independent of the advisor, in selecting an advisor, one has two parameters to assess: the frequency of having an answer to questions and the probability that an answer is correct. A function, $f(x,p) = nxp$, expresses the number of bets that I will make that are good bets, where x is the frequency of having an answer versus not, p is the probability that any given answer is true, and n the number of bets offered.[22] Any change in x or p is desirable only if $f(x,p)$ is greater as a result; hence, any change that increases the value of $f(x,p)$ is an improvement in accuracy.[23]

---

[20] To be completely precise, the odds determine the rate at which exchange of truth and falsity is rational; the present description is correct for the case in which all bets are even odds.

[21] A technical point regarding this conception involves questions with false presuppositions. To answer a question with a false presupposition implies something false (the presupposition) and therefore says something false. Moreover, any answer will say something false, so the best response is no answer at all—all answers lose a bet. Hence, we desire of our advisor the she counsels no bet in response to questions with false presuppositions.

[22] p is a simple relative frequency of truth among the advisor's beliefs.

[23] Some might claim that this isn't really accuracy, but accuracy and scope. The point seems somewhat semantic. Moreover, we need to accommodate the changes in scientific agreement that actually happen, which means we need a way to understand when the addition of new domains of study improves or harms the total accuracy of a scientific picture. Because changes in accuracy and scope almost always occur together, we need to understand changes in accuracy along with changes in scope.

An objection arises: The problem with this way of conceiving accuracy as with all such models is that it requires a prior assignment of utilities to the person selecting his advisor. In particular, in the present model, the person selecting the advisor is neither risk-averse nor risk-seeking, they are risk-neutral. If they are risk-averse, they will prefer in some cases to increase p at their own financial expense, for this will mean making fewer total bets, but more of them will be winning. If they are risk-seeking, they will prefer to increase x at their own expense, for this will mean making more total bets. Understood simply in the context of the game, risk-aversion and risk-seeking seem perplexing, but when we understand this game as a model of using science to coordinate our beliefs with the world, both seeking and avoiding risk seem like live options because mistakes may seem especially bad or agnosticism may seem especially unattractive. (As a model of the accuracy of science, perhaps risk-aversion represents avoiding error at the expense of scope, and risk-seeking represents expanding scope at the expense of error. Epistemic utilities such as these are not dictated *a priori*.)[24]

However, if the risk neutrality assumption cannot be justified, it can be eliminated. The consequence is that improved accuracy becomes vague, but the vagueness is acceptable and on par with ordinary vagueness. In certain cases risk-averse, risk-seeking, and risk-neutral individuals all agree. In these cases, we have determinate increase of accuracy. In cases where there is disagreement, we may say that it is indeterminate whether there is progress. For a fixed value of x, any increase in p is

---

[24]There is a Bayesian objection to the model that I have not discussed: according to Bayesians, I should update my probabilities on the basis of the advice of my advisor. But this just shows that the Bayesian can't make sense of deferring to authority in the way presently suggested, for once we introduce a Bayesian framework, ultimate decision rests on a function of the advisor and me, and the whole point is that I'm removing myself from the equation. The present issue seems related to the problem of modeling agnosticism for Bayesians; perhaps some Bayesian model that can incorporate agnosticism can understand the present model effectively.

Another point often made in context like the present involves Dutch Book arguments. In the present context, I think that they are an aside, since we may assume that people seeking or avoiding risk are doing so for a reason. If so, a Dutch Book only shows that there are some sequences of bets which force them to trade accuracy *for something else*, not that they will irrationally give up accuracy.

acceptable to all parties. Likewise for a fixed value of p and increasing x. Similarly, when x remains fixed and p decreases, everyone finds that unacceptable. Disagreement occurs when both x and p change: risk-seekers will accept some greater values of x with decreasing p even if $f(x,p)$ decreases provided that the total number of good bets increases, while risk-neutral and risk-averse individuals will not; risk-avoiders will accept greater values of p with decreasing x even if $f(x,p)$ decreases, while risk-neutral and risk-seeking individuals will not.[25]

The more pressing objection to this model is to say what the selection of questions amounts to. In order for this model to make sense, we have to know (even if the participants in the game do not) what the questions are, and whether some advisor is accurate or not depends on the questions we ask him, and, moreover, which changes are improvements or not depends on the questions asked. This suggests that the notion of accuracy only makes sense relative to a collection of questions.

This objection misunderstands the model. An external perspective on the model, knowing the questions that will be asked and the states of the advisor, is entirely different from the perspective within the model selecting changes to the advisor. The point of the model is to think about the accuracy of the advisor in terms of how to maximize betting potential from the perspective of the individual within the model. Consequently, the parameters of the model allow only the adjustment of advisor's belief states. In ignorance of the set of bets that will be offered, we can ask ourselves how we would want our advisor to change.[26]

The question may arise whether accuracy amounts to a form of approximate truth

---

[25]There are multiple ways to operate as a risk-seeker or risk-avoider. Each can be modeled as having a threshold of risk that they tolerate; there is more than one threshold for each sort of non-risk-neutral agent. There is no need to pursue the details of such thresholds here.

[26]As a digression from the current topic, an external perspective on the present model could be modified to represent the decisions of scientists deciding between rival research projects. In that model, we see scientists as having not only choices about advisors but interests in certain questions. Given the interest in certain questions, whether one theory or another is more accurate may be far less important than which questions the theory answers. Again, in claiming that science progresses toward accuracy, I am not claiming that accuracy is always among the desiderata for scientists selecting research projects; see page 1.2.

or truthlikeness. No doubt what I have described could be called "approximate truth," for the notion of approximate truth is antecedently quite imprecise, and the present conception of accuracy is one way to make it more precise. However, there is a prominent conception of approximate truth that differs from the present conception. According to that conception, an approximate truth says something more-or-less accurate about an actually existing thing. This notion is closely associated with scientific realism where it is applied to theories rather than statements and the central constraint is that central terms of a theory refer. (Putnam, Boyd [Boy84], Psillos [Psi99] and Maxwell [Max62] are representative of realists whose stories involve such reference. Laudan [Lau81, 230] agrees, but thinks that the history of science tells against realist inference. Chapter 3 elaborates on these issues.) The present conception of accuracy does not require such forms of reference. The present conception can allow a representation to represent light as propagating within luminiferous ether (which does not exist) and nevertheless be accurate. On certain conceptions of approximate truth (such as the one with which Laudan saddles realism), such representations are not approximately true; however, on my conception, because these representations allow one to answer many questions about light, including ones about unobservable features of light, without saying anything about a luminiferous ether, ether theories are approximately true. Consequently, mistaken ontological commitments of theories need not infect all their implications, and such theories may be called accurate (or more accurate than alternatives: see below) despite putative reference to non-existent things.[27]

---

[27]It is perhaps in the present regard that the thesis of this dissertation most differs from traditional scientific realism, which has often been associated with providing an accurate ontology of fundamental entities.

1.3.1 Models and Accuracy

I have illustrated and handled some objections regarding the increase of truth in scientific agreement. But, as I have already said, models play a critical role in science. Part of that role is representational. It will not do to ignore a central form of representation that science employs if I wish to claim that science offers an increasingly accurate picture of the world. I must now account for the development of theoretical models and explain their representational role in science. I begin with an elaboration of the use of models as representations in general; this follows Ronald Giere's presentation [Gie85][Gie88][Gie04]. Following this I discuss the notion of accuracy of models, which is particular to my own view.

Giere's example of modeling in science is from classical mechanics. Among the important models of classical mechanics is the linear oscillator. The simple harmonic oscillator is the simplest form of linear oscillator, and consists of a linear restoring force that acts on a body so as to return it to a rest position. The force is described by force function

$$F = ma = md^2x/dt^2 = -kx, \qquad (1.1)$$

which is to say that the restoring force, F is equal to a constant term k times the displacement of the restored body from its rest position, x; the negative sign indicates the the force is always in the direction of $x = 0$. Thus abstractly characterized, the simple harmonic oscillator could be regarded as a means of representing periodic motion in one dimension. The abstract mathematical structure admits of manipulations that will be informative regarding systems that are represented with it. The principle example is to solve the equations of the special cases of displacement and velocity as a function of time. In general,

$$f(t) = A\cos(wt) + B\sin(wt), \qquad (1.2)$$

where $w^2 = k/m$, and A and B are determined by the initial conditions of the system.

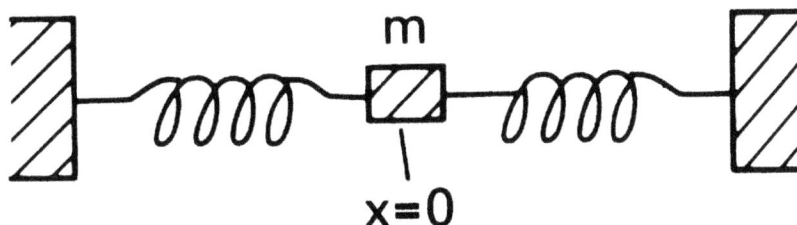

FIGURE 1.1. The Simple Harmonic Oscillator. The body in the middle, with mass m, is subject to a restoring force by the springs connected to it. Here, the position of the mass is $x = 0$, and so it is undisplaced and subject to no force. If it were displaced, it would be subject to a force equal to $-kx$. This image replicates one in Giere [Gie88, 69].

To take a concrete example, where A is the initial position and the initial velocity is 0, they are

$$x(t) = A\cos(wt) \qquad v(t) = -Aw\sin(wt). \tag{1.3}$$

Simply to describe a mathematical structure does not explain how it is a representation. Representing a system with a mathematical structure involves identifying elements of the structure with elements of a system that it is used to represent. The textbook example in the case of the linear oscillator is a mass on a spring, which is the case of Hooke's Law. In this case, k is identified with the stiffness of the spring. The force exerted by the spring is proportional to the amount that the spring is stretched. Thus, the position and velocity of the spring-mass system can be investigated by examining the properties of the simple harmonic oscillator model. This is illustrated in figure 1.1.

No physical system is a simple harmonic oscillator. Physical masses on springs come to rest; masses in simple harmonic oscillators do not. Friction due to air resistance, friction within the spring, perturbations due to gravitation, energy lost in the less-than-ideally rigid posts, the mass of the spring, and hosts of other factors all mean that no physical system accords precisely with the solutions for the simple harmonic oscillator. As a partial recognition of this fact, mechanics also offers the damped linear oscillator. The equation

$$F = ma = md^2x/dt^2 = -kx + bv \qquad (1.4)$$

gives the force function that describes the damped oscillator. This equation is the one that we had for simple harmonic oscillation, but with additional term, bv, which is a function of velocity, v. The amplitude of motion of the damped linear oscillator decreases with time (unlike the linear oscillator). In a standard use, the constant b represents the frictional force that damps the motion of the physical mass. Of course, this model does not deliver us from unaccounted forces. Some of those above mentioned will remain present, and friction itself is merely a heuristic for billions of particle interactions.

Models employed in mechanics, as elsewhere in science, are idealizations. We identify components of abstract mathematical structures with components of real physical systems.[28] Because this is something we do, representation of systems with models is not an intrinsic feature of the models themselves. Linguistic descriptions are often taken to have meanings independent of their particular use. But models do not have meanings. Rather, scientists *use* models to represent systems by forming hypotheses about models and physical systems. Models, when they are successful, are similar to the things that scientists model with them.[29] Scientists specify within their theoretical hypotheses respects and degrees of similarities; these similarities are what allow scientists to use the models to represent the systems that they do. Note that similarity does not make the model representational; it is the use of the models and the explicit drawing of comparison between models that creates the representation.

---

[28]Sometimes, of course, we identify the structures with alleged components of physical systems. Theoretical hypotheses are often literally hypotheses, and views about physical systems are largely informed by models on the supposition that reality corresponds to them.

[29]In [van80], van Fraassen says the essential relationship is isomorphism. However, models are almost never isomorphic to the systems they are used to represent. So far as I know, he has abandoned this particular commitment of his earlier work; a revision to similarity seems minor. His more recent work [van08] emphasizes the pragmatic dimension of representation, and I have sympathies with its less empiricist components.

Some example of theoretical hypotheses include:

> The position and velocity of this mass-spring system over short intervals of time is very close to that of a simple harmonic oscillator.
>
> The position and velocity of this (very same) mass-spring system is very close to that of a damped harmonic oscillator.
>
> The force of friction on this mass on a spring is close to the difference bv between the damped and simple harmonic oscillators.[30]

Note that in each case, the model relates to a particular system and the claim of similarity is between the model and a particular system: such uses do not account for scientific generalizations.[31] A familiar example of scientific generalization is Hooke's Law; "laws" such as Hooke's are not exceptionless generalizations. Giere's view of such generalizations is to take them as literally true—of the model. Qualifications, which on a more syntactic view of the generalizations need to be regarded as *ceteris paribus* clauses, are instead regarded as qualifications on the application of the model. Hence, a certain restricted class of masses on springs resemble, in (perhaps tacitly) specified degrees and respects, simple harmonic oscillators, and that is the content of Hooke's law.[32]

It is worth mentioning before proceeding that the specification of respects and degrees is important and, in general, models contain structure that is not similar to the things modeled with them while things modeled contain structure that is not included in all of their models. A nice example (from Giere [Gie04, 479]) is that

---

[30] These particular examples are mine, not Giere's. His own example is the similarity between the earth and moon and a two-particle Newtonian gravitational system. [Gie88, 81] In [Gie04, 747-48], he uses the example of a mass on a spring in a way that mirrors theoretical hypotheses as discussed here.

[31] In his discussion in [Gie88], Giere does not treat generalization. However, [Gie04] elaborates on generalizations and laws.

[32] This is the *representational* content of Hooke's law; Hooke's law, and other laws, should also be regarded as a sort of recipe for constructing models of physical systems, which could be regarded as a sort of content. Being a recipe is certainly a role of Hooke's law, whether that role gives it "content" in some sense or not.

water is often modeled as a continuous fluid. But bodies of water are dissimilar from continuous fluids, for example, in being collections of discrete particles, i.e., by not being continuous fluids at all. But that is fine: a body of water resembles a continuous fluid in a number of specifiable respects and that is what's necessary to represent certain behavior of the water. This fact will be important as we consider the notion of accuracy below.

Science progresses when the accuracy of its representations improves, so there is something that can be said about the accuracy of models. However, I suspect there is nothing to be said regarding the intrinsic accuracy of models. The position of a particle in a model has a position 3.12 meters different from the system it's used to represent—is that accurate or inaccurate? Obviously, context has a lot to do with this judgment, and one wonders what it would mean to say that this is objectively accurate or inaccurate. One thing that is relevant here is scale: 3.12m is terrible for a small pendulum, pretty good for a cannon ball and incredible for a planet. I'm skeptical that this can be worked into an absolute standard of accuracy, but the point is moot since scale is not a generally applicable standard for assessing the accuracy of models. Models of the structure of DNA, bacteria population growth, the spread of bird flu don't have any obvious objective interpretation in terms of scale. Once we consider using a model for some particular purpose, what is and is not accurate becomes clearer, but it also ceases to be objective: what is accurate for one purpose is not for another.

However, an absolute scale of accuracy is no more necessary to the investigation of scientific models than was an absolute scale of temperature to the early study of heat. Relative comparisons of models offer objective characterization of accuracy, and, because scientific progress is a matter of relations between stages of science, that is all that we need. A deviation of 3.12 meters is more accurate than 3.12 light years and less accurate than 3.12 angstroms. Thus, a representation of x with a model m is more accurate in respect r than a representation of x with another model m' if the similarity of m to x in respect r is greater than the similarity of m' to x in respect r; if m is at least as accurate in every respect and more accurate in some, m is more accurate than m' *simpliciter*.

1.3.2 Objections from Fundamental Physics

At one point in time, I hoped to display successive increases in accuracy in early models of quantum theory from Bohr to Schrödinger, with particular attention to models of hydrogen atoms. The largest barrier to doing so seems to be the lack of an emerging agreement among physicists regarding the interpretation of quantum mechanics. Einstein and Schrödinger remained opponents of the Copenhagen interpretation to the end of their days. Principal advocates of the Copenhagen interpretation, Bohr and Heisenberg, maintained rather different understandings of that interpretation, and Bohr in particular was often equivocal. The Copenhagen interpretation has been variously associated with Bohr's principle of Complementarity, Heisenberg's uncertainty relations, Born's probabilistic interpretation of Schrödinger's wave mechanics, and admixtures of all of these [Ste08]. Steward [Ste08, 145] aptly describes "agreement" among the advocates of the Copenhagen interpretation as an "ill-defined accommodation of apparently conflicting views."

Consequently, there appears to be a lack of agreement regarding quantum mechanics beyond an appreciation of a mathematical formalism and its use in particular problems. For example, agreement emerges that the Schrödinger equation coupled with a suitable potential energy function allows one to derive the Rydberg constant for the Balmer series in a way that makes quantization emerge naturally, and the ordinary choice for doing so makes potential energy a function of the radius of the orbit, $-e^2/r$. But little agreement emerges over how to interpret that function because little agreement emerges regarding orbits, which understood realistically (but implausibly) would be continuous spatial paths about the nucleus.

All of this is compatible with my view: accuracy need not improve in any particular way to be considered progressive, and so the local improvements in representations, such as of the energies of electrons, if not their orbits, is enough. It is compatible with the progress of science, on my view, that we never discover the structure of the atom. Richard Healey has objected to my view that subsequent models of quantum theory don't reveal similar respects r of comparison, and my account of accuracy thus founders. But I believe I can offer a two-fold response to this objection. First, it seems to me that subsequent models lack uniform interpretation among physicists, and that, consequently, no agreement emerges. Because we assess the accuracy of agreement and there is no agreement, little prevents me from saying that fully interpreted quantum mechanics is not a topic about which science has yet made progress. Nevertheless, more local forms of progress are real: although scientists seem to have no interpretation of the formalism that makes it represent any features of reality, scientists are able to produce representations of particular systems using the formalism. Recall that my notion of accuracy does not require us to have referring terms within our theories; insofar as successive quantum mechanical models of, for example, hydrogen allow us to answer more questions about hydrogen, and to answer them more accurately, our science improves regarding accuracy, even if an interpretation of the formalism is unavailable.

Successive models of quantum mechanics seem to reject certain questions about hydrogen (and nature more generally) because those questions are based on false presuppositions.[33] This seems correct to me, but it is no threat to the present conception of accuracy, since questions that depend upon false presuppositions have no answers (true or false). Moreover, if the community correctly appreciates that certain questions have false presuppositions, that in itself is discovery and will count toward the increasing accuracy of the community's agreement.

---

[33] Richard Healey pointed this out in comments on an earlier version of this chapter.

1.4 The Project

In chapter 2, I discuss the development of science and the typical process of agreement formation therein. The process, I argue, is one of reaching agreement through convergence rather than consensus: scientists exhibit significant cognitive diversity so that their acceptance occurs from idiosyncratic considerations that vary from scientist to scientist rather than from uniform, shared considerations. Consequently, scientific results emerge from and despite considerable differences in the reasoning of various scientists whose acceptance constitutes scientific agreements. I illustrate these features of scientific development through a discussion of the plate tectonic revolution in geosciences. The merits of this cognitive diversity considerably improve the capacity of scientific groups regarding both the discovery and certification of scientific theories; chapter 2 handles the issue of discovery.

Chapter 3 turns to the contribution of diversity to certification of scientific theories. (For present purposes, certification amounts to demonstration of accuracy.) As a result of agreeing by convergence, the process of scientific agreement is best explained by the accuracy of the representations that scientists uniformly accept. The convergent agreement is a certifying process. However, it does so merely contrastively, by altering agreement only when a more accurate alternative is available to scientists. This assures the more-or-less monotonic increase in the accuracy of science. I contrast my view with that of traditional scientific realism, and I respond to the most important objection to the explanatory defense of realism, the pessimistic induction. The pessimistic induction is a direct challenge to the realist's inference from instrumental success to truth, and consequently a challenge to the form of explanatory defense that I offer. However, the pessimistic induction is unsuccessful because it fails to show that the best historical cases of successful science enjoy success comparable to the most successful contemporary scientific theories. I contrast a favorite topic of the pessimistic induction, caloric, with a modern scientific success, oxygen, and show that the success of caloric, though considerable, in no way rivals that of oxygen: the realists' general inference is thus unthreatened, even if it is slightly weakened.

Chapters 4 and 5 discuss certain rival conceptions of scientific progress. In chapter 4, I consider the idea that science has certain aims and that scientific progress amounts to the successful fulfillment of its aims. However, I argue that science has no aims; this result follows from the fact that the cognitive diversity of science belies attributing any aim to the community, while the norms of scientific practice, insofar as there are any, admit of multiple explanations in terms of aims. Aims, moreover, seem to constitute a ground for the normative appraisal of scientists; if they do, then much of the cognitive diversity that I praise becomes unscientific. It is thus part of the evaluative picture that I espouse that science has no aims. Chapter 5 turns to arguments from Alexander Bird claiming that scientific progress is the accumulation of knowledge. I argue that he is incorrect. First, his main arguments that science aims at knowledge are unsatisfactory. More importantly, conceiving scientific progress in terms of knowledge obfuscates developmental processes within science.

Chapter 2

Justifying Agreement

In this chapter, I argue that the development and growth of science results from processes that increase its accuracy. The root of these processes is significant cognitive diversity, i.e., diversity among scientists regarding how they accept representations as accurate. The concomitant process of agreement is one of convergence; an agreement is one of convergence, roughly speaking, when each party to the agreement reaches it from independent reasons. I explain the notions of cognitive diversity and convergence in §2.1, and in §2.2 I illustrate them through a discussion of the revolution in geological science regarding continental mobility. In the final section (§2.3), I argue that scientific justification and discovery profit from diversity. §2.1 and §2.2 thus explain and illustrate the processes that increase the accuracy of science, while §2.3 explains how these processes increase accuracy; the discussion of increasing accuracy continues in chapter 3, where I relate the present considerations of diversity and convergence to the explanatory defense of realism.

2.1 Diversity and Convergence

Scientific communities exhibit a significant amount of cognitive diversity. Cognitive diversity includes differences in how scientists reason about problems. Differences in reasoning about problems include (1) differences in assessments of problem solutions and (2) differences in ways of seeking solutions. (To put these two differences in familiar terms, these are differences in what scientists count as justified and differences in how they attempt to discover solutions.) Cognitive diversity also includes (3) differences in the problems that scientists attempt to solve, and (4) their assessments of the merits of solving particular problems. Finally, cognitive diversity includes (5) differences in what scientists accept.

Thus understanding cognitive diversity means that we understand individual scientists as involving five different factors that influence their decisions; for convenience, we may label a collection of these factors a *perspective*. Cognitive diversity does not exhaust the varieties of diversity, but it does exhaust the variety of diversity that is directly relevant to scientific decision making.[1] Of course, certain variations among scientists may be *sources* of cognitive diversity: education, socio-economic background, national origin, ethnicity, political affiliation, and gender probably influence these five factors. Indeed, it may be that a certain perspectives are only achieved by individuals with particular backgrounds.[2] Whether this is so is a contingent, empirical matter not to be decided in the present work. This *personal diversity* is likely an able proxy for cognitive diversity, but personally diverse groups are not *ipso facto* cognitively diverse.[3]

Agreement must be a central topic of concern for understanding scientific progress, and the influence of diversity on agreement is significant. Agreement forms when scientists uniformly accept something, but the process of acceptance need not be identical in all scientists. Indeed, in prototypical cases, agreement results from scientists reasoning differently to the same conclusion; this is the obvious effect of cognitive diversity upon scientific agreement. The reasoning processes that engender acceptance are diverse, and consequently, what scientists accept will ordinarily be diverse. Scientific agreement is a special case of diverse processes converging on some

---

[1] I take myself to be advancing a thesis about cognitive diversity, and articulating or clarifying that notion in terms of these five factors. There are alternative articulations of cognitive diversity, but I suspect that my thesis about cognitive diversity would also apply to the notion alternatively articulated.

[2] It is obviously a highly controversial matter whether certain perspectives require having a certain personal background, i.e., for example, whether scientific communities comprising only men (to pick a salient historical example) will *necessarily* lack certain perspectives.

[3] Here I differ somewhat in my treatment of diversity from Miriam Solomon, who does not always separate perspectives, which are proximate causal factors in decisions, and sources of perspectives, which are distal causal factors in decisions.

particular representation.[4] Of course, it is possible that scientists reach agreement for a uniform reason, but it is unusual.

This account of scientific development is at odds with much philosophical tradition. According to that tradition, science develops in response to the appreciation of reasons and that appreciation is uniform in the scientific community. Not every version of this traditional view has been equally stringent. The strongest and probably oldest says that science employs a method which, when coupled with appropriate information, yields acceptance. Thus, the production of agreement in scientific communities involves the successful distribution of relevant information so that individual scientists see that application of the method yields a decision regarding a certain representation. Some philosophers have weakened that; rather than seeking a method, they make a weaker claim: agreement results when overwhelming reasons prevail, but reasoning may vary from one episode to another. This weaker version allows that different representations may be accepted as accurate on different types of bases, but requires that each representation be accepted for a uniform reason. Thus, population biology and optics might be methodologically different, so that the structure of reasoning in population biology differs from that of optics. However, scientific agreement in population biology occurs when population biologists appreciate the reason for accepting some representation. Even more liberally, some people allow that even within a given science there may be methodological diversity, so that two representations p and q might be accepted in structurally, methodologically distinct ways, P and Q. Nevertheless, agreement about p occurs because (roughly speaking) scientists see that P is the reason for p. I call these traditional philosophical pictures the *consensus model* of scientific development. Characteristic of a consensus model of scientific development is the idea that agreement is driven by engaging in a common

---

[4]Throughout this chapter I am concerned with acceptance of a representation as accurate; however, I suspect that much of what I say could be said about other types of acceptance as well, although those other types of acceptance may offer no sense in which accuracy is part of the account.

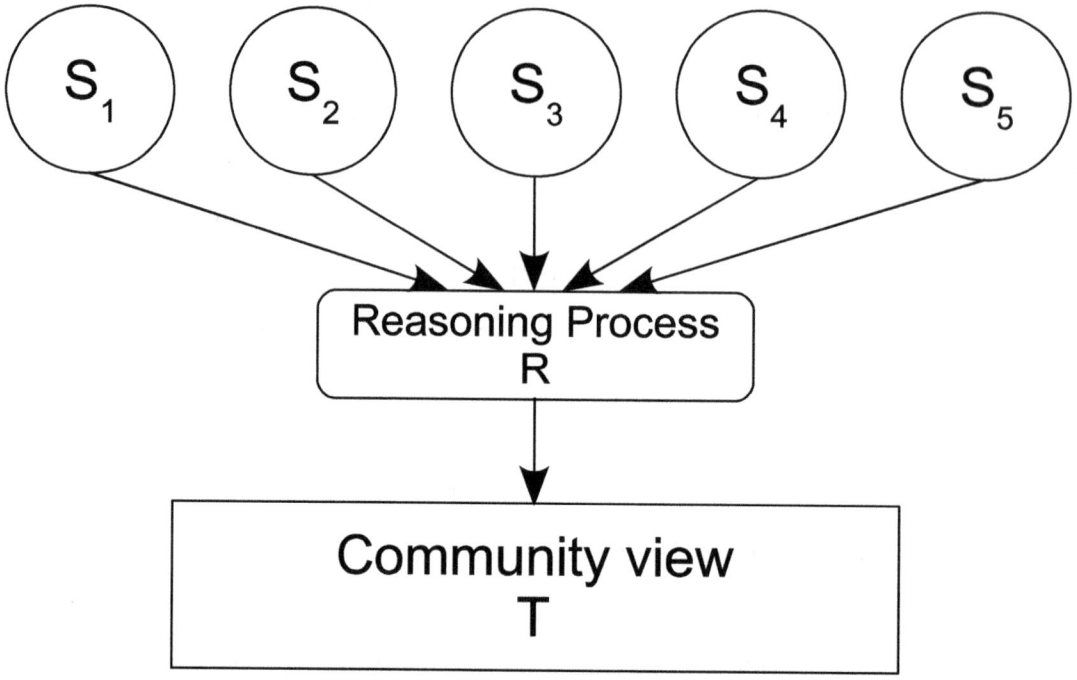

FIGURE 2.1. The consensus model of scientific development. Disagreement resolves and debate ends when scientists (or sub-communities of scientists), S_i, uniformly accept a reason as supporting what becomes the agreed upon view of the community, T.

psychological process. The consensus model is schematically depicted in figure 2.1.

Cognitive diversity does not favor development according to a consensus model, but what I call the *convergence model* of scientific development. What is characteristic of the convergence model is that there are diverse psychological processes, instantiated in different scientists, when they come to agree about some representation. Roughly speaking, when a group of scientists, $s_1 \ldots s_n$, agrees about some representation, p, each scientist has a perspective that leads her to accept p, and no two perspectives are the same. This may be a bit extreme, but typical cases will reveal many perspectives that lead to accepting p—not, as a consensus model suggests, merely one. The convergence model is schematically depicted in figure 2.2.

Agreements that fit the convergence model are widespread. If you believe that

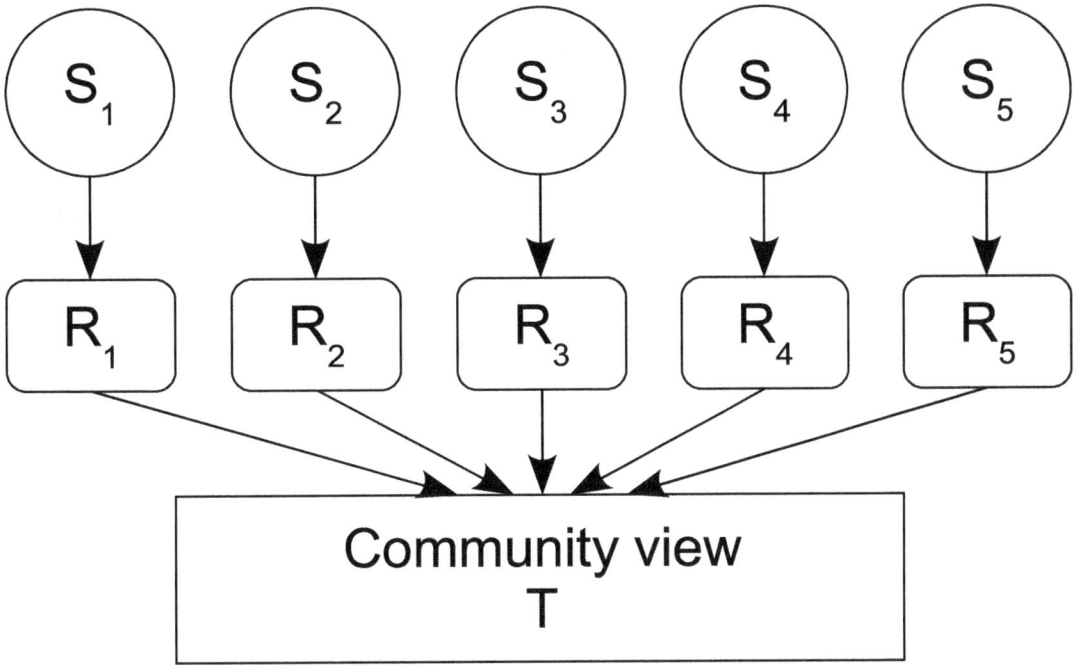

FIGURE 2.2. The convergence model of scientific development. When agreement forms, it does so because individual scientists or sub-communities of scientists, S_i, engage distinctive psychological processes, R_i, that lead them to accept what becomes the agreed upon view of the community, T.

environmental concerns are critical and I believe that civil liberties are critical but we both vote for the same candidate, our agreement about that candidate fits a convergence model. If you desire a healthy dinner and I desire a tasty one but we agree that salmon is the best option, our agreement fits a convergence model. If you and I believe that a particular pitcher will improve this season—you, because he has about 400 innings of major league experience and is well regarded by scouts, I because he underperformed expectations based on his past peripheral statistics—our agreement fits a convergence model.[5]

---

[5] Advanced statistical techniques reveal that an analysis of pitcher performance based on his strikeout, walk and groundball rates is a far better predictor of future runs allowed than his past runs allowed are. For example, $QERA = (2.69 - 3.40K\% + 3.88BB\% - 0.66GB\%)^2 \approx ERA$. Strikeout rate and so forth are often called "peripheral stats".

Consensus models of agreement formation seem to have dominated philosophical discussions of agreement. This is certainly true of philosophy of science before Kuhn.[6] Even since Kuhn, realist and anti-realist philosophers of science have alleged to identify a sole source of scientific decision making. Even those philosophers of science, such as Kitcher, who have emphasized social processes and individual idiosyncrasies in scientific development have nevertheless endorsed a consensus model of development. (An important exception to this rule is Larry Laudan, who argues that others have fallaciously understood scientific development by assuming (in his terms) that scientific disagreements at the level of fact, method, or value must be occasioned by, and must occasion, disagreements at another level. Laudan thus sees other philosophers (in my terms) as assigning widely shared perspectives to "sides" in scientific debates, rather than appreciating the diversity of perspectives that typically join each side. See [Lau84].[7])

According to Kitcher, scientific communities self-organize to achieve the impersonal epistemic goals of the community. The locus of Kitcher's consensus model of scientific development is in his discussion of scientific disagreement. Kitcher believes that the resolution of scientific disagreements is an extended process that ultimately concludes as a result of articulating decisive arguments. Kitcher sets up his account as a synthesis of rationalist and anti-rationalist accounts.[8] Rationalism, according to Kitcher, embodies five theses: First, community decision occurs when all individuals within the community have independently made the same modification of their

---

[6]Kuhn's philosophical view in *Structure of Scientific Revolutions* is a consensus model, for in that picture, paradigms dominate the psychology of scientists and paradigm shifts are essentially changes in the dominance of paradigm; in later work, Kuhn seems to adopt a convergence view (see §2.3 below.)

[7]See also fn. 4, ch. 3

[8]Rationalism and anti-rationalism are not particular views, but themes common to two strands of philosophy in the twentieth century. The dichotomy is artificial, but it is also helpful in making clear which elements of different philosophies Kitcher's synthesis involves. From the outset, Kitcher proposes to offer a view that avoids the excesses of "Legend" while avoiding the rival excess of anti-rationalism, which, in Kitcher's view, throws out the baby with the bath water.

practice[9]; each member of the community is moved solely by the epistemic goal of modifying practice so as to achieve the impersonal epistemic goals of the community; all members of the community start with the same practice and receive the same stimuli; while there is debate in the community, champions of the modification that ultimately triumphs succeed because their modification is superior to their rivals; debate closes when those who champion the inferior practice change their practice and adopt the superior one of their rivals [Kit93, 196-7].[10]

Anti-rationalism, by contrast, embodies five alternative theses: community decision is reached when enough sub-groups of scientists elect a certain modification of practice; scientists are typically motivated by non-epistemic as well as epistemic goals; scientists exhibit significant variation in their individual practices; during all phases of scientific debate, neither the victors nor the losers engage a superior practice; scientific debates are closed when one group musters sufficient power to exclude their rivals.[11]

Kitcher's own view is a synthesis of these two. He accepts certain anti-rationalist ideas about scientific development: scientists are motivated by epistiemic and non-epistemic concerns; scientific communities exhibit significant cognitive variation; and agreement occurs when sufficiently many powerful sub-groups within the community assent. But he contends that, during the process of scientific debate, one side may develop superior practices, so that the changes which that side advocates are more suited to progress than those of their rivals; moreover, scientific debates close because of the articulation and acceptance of decisive arguments; as he puts it:

> Scientific debates are closed when, as a result of conversations among

---

[9]'Practice' is a technical term for Kitcher; it incorporates the host of psychological features of a scientist that affect his research, not only in terms of its outcomes, but also what he decides to research, and the rest of it. Kitcher never acknowledges the distinction between convergence and consensus processes.

[10]Kitcher actually devotes an entire section of [Kit93] to the metaphors of war that he employs.

[11]Kitcher adds to this final condition that the superior processes are the beneficiaries of subsequent research effort so that subsequent historical evaluation tends to reveal a highly successful research project in contrast with an underdeveloped rival.

> peers and encounters with nature that are partially produced by early decisions to modify individual practices, there emerges in the community a widely available argument, encapsulating a process for modifying practice which... is markedly superior in promoting cognitive progress than other processes undergone by protagonists in the debate; power accrues to the victorious group principally in virtue of the integration of this process into the thinking of members of the community and recognition of its virtues. [Kit93, 201]

Thus, according to Kitcher, when scientific disagreements are resolved, certain psychological processes rule the day; the ultimate topic of agreement is successful *because* of those psychological processes.

Kitcher includes diversity as an important part of scientific development because it plays an important role in creating divisions of labor that conduce to the epistemic goals of the community.[12] Divisions of labor assure the scientific communities invest their resources so as to find important scientific results, and also help to ensure that the community delivers criticisms and responses to criticisms that are essential to fully developing science. However, Kitcher's view effectively limits the role of diversity to scientific discovery, not justification. For Kitcher, diversity influences division of labor (and possibly cognitive search space as well) so as to improve the community's ability to *seek* solutions. Even as regards delivery of criticism and response, diversity is essentially involved in seeking justification. Ultimately, for Kitcher, convergence is out of the picture, and the ultimate *justificatory* story is no different than if a single scientist had spun the final product, whole cloth, without any community involvement whatsoever.

In several respects, I agree with Kitcher's picture of scientific communities. An important contrast between Kitcher's psychologically and socially complex account of

---

[12]I deny that the community has such goals; see chapter 4.

scientific development and my own, however, involves the role of diversity in generating agreements: Kitcher favors consensus, I favor convergence. According to Kitcher, psychologism is the critical step in producing a plausible account of scientific development, and his view becomes a potentially tractable form of rationalism once we eliminate the artificial psychology of traditional rationalism. My view says that socialization is the essential step, and critical work (both as discovery and justification) is done by the convergent, social process of agreement formation. The complexity Kitcher introduces allows an *a posteriori* method which undergoes changes as science makes factual and theoretical advances; in part, scientists discover this method through their social interaction. Nevertheless, the method itself is individually manifest, and it is the method that certifies scientific results. My view allows factual and theoretical advances to shape individual scientific perspectives, and allows that individual perspectives develop, in part, through social interaction. However, over and above these individual perspectives, the scientific community certifies scientific results in a process that is communally rather than individually manifest.

Kitcher can't avail himself of this socialization within his consensus model, for his consensus model simply manifests individual activity at the social level. In order to avail ourselves of socialized justifications, we must reject consensus models. If there is anything to a social epistemological process—a process that outstrips individual belief formation—consensus models have to be rejected. A main question, of course, is whether scientific processes socialize justification. The remainder of this chapter reveals diversity and convergence in scientific communities through an example (§2.2) and then argues that diversity and convergence improve scientific communities (§2.3).

With a few exceptions (Laudan [Lau84], later Kuhn [Kuh77], and possibly Solomon [Sol01]), philosophers of science have not recognized the presence of convergence in scientific agreements, and this occurs in spite of more widespread recognition of cognitive diversity. I should at least offer a diagnosis of this situation. One possible cause for neglecting convergence is that convergence involves disagreement about reasons for belief, and philosophers are suspicious of beliefs absent agreement about reasons for belief. Another possible reason is the tendency of philosophers of science to characterizes scientific debates in terms of sides; this leads us to over-emphasize the allegiance of members of sides, i.e., the ways in which they agree, while disagreements that we emphasize are ones that divide the two sides. Moreover, seeing debates in terms of sides tends to emphasize events that cause parties to switch allegiances while under-emphasizing factors (perspectives) that are a necessary background for the events to alter allegiances. Consequently, we *see* disagreement as belonging to the debate and agreement as belonging to allegiances, and we see events as having an evidential role independently of the perspectives of scientists. The detailed study of geoscience in the next section reveals a more subtle situation.

2.2 Geological Science and Scientific Development

A terminological note is in order before discussing the revolution in geosciences. First, terminology for geological science is ordinarily somewhat ambiguous; 'geology' is sometimes use to encompass all or many of the subfields, including geophysics, seismology, oceanography, and so forth, but it is also used for the specific study of rock formations, as distinct from these other specializations. I use the term 'geological science' or 'geoscience' to encompass the the broad field and reserve 'geology' for the narrower specialized subfield.

The revolution in the geological sciences is not about one idea. As in any substantial scientific change, many representations are involved. It is natural to characterize the evolution as a debate between two sides, one of which believed continents move, the other of which denied that. But the shared commitments of each side were an evolving collection of representations.[13] Some of the nuances of these collections will emerge below. Here it is important to mention three different ideas that capture some

---

[13]The talk of sides is, I think, somewhat misleading, for it tempts us to think that most scientists were active participants in a debate. Many geoscientists were not active participants.

of the broadest commitments in the revolution. Continental drift is Wegener's hypothesis that continents are separate slabs of rock that move on top of the sea-floor. Sea-floor spreading is the idea that the Earth's crust is composed of separate slabs that float on a molten core and whose boundaries are under-sea ridges. Mobilism is the idea that continents exhibit motions relative to one another; it subsumes the various proposals of the ultimately victorious side.[14]

The story of plate tectonics begins with Wegener's 1915 book *The Origin of Continents and Oceans*.[15] In it, he proposed that continents can move around on the ocean floor much like glaciers move around on land. His evidence for the view was limited to explanatory results that include several geological similarities between Africa and South America, the topological fit between South America's eastern coast and Africa's western one, and the fossil record. In each case, there are important similarities between Africa and South America.

Despite some handsome arguments, Wegener's work attracted few adherents. Most geoscientists expressed no opinion at all, but expressed opinions were largely negative. Three sources of argument were prominent among Wegener's critics. First, several scientists reacted to the alleged fit between coast lines. These arguments are somewhat equivocal, since they come in two kinds: the first contend that the fit is too perfect; because the lateral motion of the continents would have severely eroded the edges of the continents, we would not expect to find a fit between Africa and South America if they had once been adjacent to one another. The second argument about fit was that the the fit was not good at all; Charles Schuckert famously cut South America out of a globe and lined it up against the coast of Africa to point out that there are several sites where the continents line up poorly. Paleontological arguments were rejected because many researchers claimed to find similar fossil

---

[14]The term "mobilism" is due to Ronald Giere [Gie88].

[15]Similar ideas had been proposed by catastrophist geoscientists in the 1800s, which contributed to some hostile responses to Wegener's work. In the 20th century, Wegener's is the first drift hypothesis to receive attention.

similarities in parts other parts of the globe. Finally, geophysical arguments were offered to show that the amount of force necessary to move the continents would be far beyond anything available to have moved them. Harold Jeffreys, who did not accept mobilism until the 1970's, offered several such arguments that gave precise mathematical calculations of the force necessary to move continents.

There were a handful of converts to Wegener's ideas. Notably, geologists whose field work included the southern hemisphere and alpine geologists were much more likely than others to be persuaded of Wegener's drift hypothesis, or at least to take mobilism seriously. Alexander du Toit's 1937 *Our Wandering Continents* was a lengthy book that asserted Wegener's ideas, but he elaborated on the evidence and corrected some of Wegener's mistakes. Although this refined version of continental drift improved on Wegener's picture, it does not appear to have generated new converts outside alpine and southern hemisphere geologists. Arthur Holmes, one of the most prominent British geoscientists of his day, proposed a geophysical model of the earth's mantle in 1929; that model could account for drift, and that model resembles those which ultimately accompanied the drift hypothesis in the 1960's, but Holmes himself accepted the model without accepting a particular variation in which drift did occur [Ste90]. The state of play regarding mobilism remained mostly unchanged until the 1950's. A handful of converts to Wegener's thesis detailed further arguments similar to his, but no especially new ideas regarding mobilism emerged until the 1950's.

Geophysicists working on data regarding the earth's magnetic fields offered the first evidence different in kind from that of Wegener. Rocks around the world sometimes exhibit a feature known as natural remnant magnetism; when molten, the molecules in rocks naturally orient themselves to the earth's magnetic field. Provided that they solidify at the right temperatures, the rocks will retain a magnetic alignment. As a consequence, if continents are mobile, it is possible that rocks move so that they no longer align with the orientation of the magnetic field where they are found. The discovery of rocks whose remnant magnetism did not fit with polar orientations suggested to several geophysicists that the continents moved.

On the basis of such observation, paleomagneticists headed by Patrick Blackett publish an article concluding that India had moved 4,000 miles from the southern hemisphere to its present location over the last 125 million years. In 1956, another paleomagneticist, Keith Runcorn, published a paper rejecting Blackett's group's findings. Runcorn was actually a student of Harold Jeffries, the geophysicist who offered the most precise geophysical arguments against continental drift. However, later in 1956, Runcorn recanted and came to support mobilism for reasons similar to Blackett's.

Many geologists drew attention to several assumptions that Runcorn and Blackett relied upon, and also doubted some of the techniques that they used. The process of removing magnetically remnant rocks disturbs their magnetic properties and a cleaning process was used after they were extracted. Moreover, statistical averages rather than individual measurements were used to draw conclusions about remnant magnetism. These two facts, as well as others, raised concerns, and geoscientists outside paleomagneticists were unconvinced by the evidence that was offered.

Mapping of the world's ocean floor after World War Two drew the attention of geological scientists to the series of ridges that trace their way around the world's ocean basins. If one begins in the Arctic ocean, one can trace a ridge all the way to the mid-Atlantic to the tip of Africa, then through the Indian ocean, past Australia and finally to up the Pacific along the coasts of North America and into Alaska. In response to this information about the ocean floors, Harry Hess published a new geophysical model of the earth's crust and interior in 1962 and 1963; his model is a mobilist one and a key to subsequent mobilist developments.[16]

Hess's geophysical model proposes that the outer layer of the earth rests on a

---

[16]Robert Dietz was the first to publish (in 1961) a hypothesis of sea-floor spreading; however, Dietz acknowledged that a presentation by Hess in 1960 was influential and he credits Hess with priority.

molten core in which there are powerful convection currents. Where the currents are rising, ridges are forming, and where they are falling, trenches and mountain ranges form. Swirling convection currents in the earths's interior push up here in the middle, creating the ridge. As a result of the convection current underneath, which travels away from the ridge, the slabs of lithosphere are also pulled away from the ridge and into each other at the trenches.

Hess's model has some explanatory merits. First, it explains why sea-floor sediments tend to be thicker near continents and thin at the ridges. Second, it explains why no ocean basin had ever been dated more than 180 million years old. Third, it explained some data regarding seismic activity. Hess didn't invent the idea of a molten core or anything as dramatic as that; in a number of respects, his model is much like others in its day.

In 1963, Fred Vine and Drummond Mathews hypothesized that sea-floor spreading and magnetic reversals of the earth's poles could combine to explain the known pattern of magnetic bands in the sea floor. In the late fifties, studies of natural remnant magnetism in the earth's floor revealed that remnant magnetism in the ocean floor tended to create a pattern of bands: long narrow strips of one polarity adjacent to long narrow strips of opposite polarity. If sea-floors are spreading and the Earth's magnetic field periodically reverses (neither idea was widely accepted at the time) then a such a system of bands is to be expected. Of special importance was a later development: that the linear magnetic bands should be symmetrical about a ridge. In 1965, Matthews tested this hypothesis and argued that it was correct. The thought was controversial among oceanographers, and several publications argued that his results were unconvincing. However, within about one year, several results of a similar nature reversed opinions, and many oceanographers came to accept sea-floor spreading as a result.

J. Tuzo Wilson, a student of Harry Hess, dedicated most of his research from 1960 onward to investigating the implications of sea-floor spreading. He was actually responsible for noting the implication that the magnetic bands should be symmetrical about ocean ridges. A further important contribution of his was a theory of transform faults. Within ocean ridges there are unusual breaks perpendicular to the ridge, so that rather than being perfectly continuous there are little jumps perpendicular to the ridge that interrupt their nearly continuous path. Wilson called these "transform faults" and suggested a mechanism for their formation that amended Hess's sea-floor spreading model. Wilson's account of transform faults accompanied data from magnetic studies of sea-floor that the various transform faults were formed by the same processes. The hypothesis also lead Wilson to propose that there is a large continuous network of belts around the earth that divide its surface into a collection of rigid plates.

The result through 1966 was that a significant proportion of geophysicsists and oceanographers were convinced of sea-floor spreading. The symmetry of the magnetic profiles and their use in predicting the age of various parts of the sea-floor were quite influential. Many geoscientists were still unconvinced, but by 1966 mobilism enjoyed a fairly large following among geoscientists. Citation studies in [Ste90] show a marked jump in references to papers on sea-floor spreading in 1967.

Plate Tectonics develops in the wake of the oceanographic results of the mid-1960s. Whereas previous work on geophysics of the earth had focused on the mechanisms of plate motion and relating these mechanisms of hypothetical convection currents, plate tectonics concerned itself solely with the kinematics of plate motions. In my opinion, this is a crucial detail that other philosophers have been too ready to ignore. Plate Tectonics completes mobilism as Newton completes heliocentrism. Identifying sea-floor spreading with the critical point in mobilism would be like calling Kepler the terminus of heliocentrism. Kepler's contribution was critical, just as sea-floor spreading was critical. Nevertheless, Kepler's account needed a mechanism. Roughly speaking, Newton provided it. Likewise, it's all well and good to say that continents move and understand a mechanism whereby they do so, but there's a further critical step: to describe in a precise way what those motions are like.[17]

The principal developers of early plate tectonics were seismologists. Plate tectonics identified three sorts of plate boundaries (ridges, trenches, and transform faults), and seismic data was essential to predicting and calculating the motions of plates at the transform fault boundaries. A large amount of seismic data was also integrated into the mobilist model and given a new interpretation.

The application of mobilist ideas to continental geology was slower than in other areas. From 1968 onward, there are studies that gradually introduce mobilist ideas in continental geology, but the advance is much less rapid than the integration of mobilism in oceanography and seismology from 1965–1968. Geologists who had accepted mobilism (a small minority) developed models of mountain formation that reinterpreted the previous account, known as geosyncline theory. The major features of mountain formation, they contended, could be understood in terms of the interaction of continental plates. However, these attempts from 1968 to 1970 were poorly received.

Several changes were important to continental geologists' acceptance of mobilism. One of them was development of advanced plate tectonic models that did not assume that the plates are rigid. If plate are rigid, their interest holds largely for those whose research includes the boundaries where all the action happens, and those boundaries are mostly under the ocean. It's not especially pertinent to continental geology. During the 1970, the relaxation of this assumption and its application to mountain formation made mobilism relevant to continental geologists.

Perhaps the most important development for continental geology was prediction of phenomena known as "exotic terranes" [Ste90]. Tuzo Wilson suggested in a 1968 paper that while now separate continents were once adjacent, bits of one continent may have broken off and traveled with the other one. As a result, North America

---

[17]Of course, there's a disanalogy in that the temporal order of kinematic and mechanical theories is reversed in the two cases.

might include a handful of regions unusually similar to Asia. And that is exactly what was discovered. These regions of North America were relatively isolated and had been ignored or dismissed previously. Mobilism offered a solution to this state of affairs. It turns out that these regions were individually small, but that a significant portion of North America is actually composed of these exotic terranes from different eras. Additionally, alterations of basic ideas about mountain formations developed in the early 1980s were important to theories of how mountains such as the Andes might have formed. According to those views, such mountains are partially exotic terranes formed by the collisions of plates.

As we reflect on this revolution in geological science, it becomes clear that the parties involved did not share reasons or motivations for accepting mobilism. The psychological causes of acceptance were not the same in every case. Indeed, causes of acceptance in one scientist were not always similarly efficacious in another. Scientific acceptance is not merely a matter of being in different places at different times; scientists in similar situations make incompatible judgments.

However, the acceptance of mobilism exhibits a pattern: There was little substantial shift in the proportion of drift advocates until the mid-50's when several geophysicists on the basis of magnetic data became convinced that continents move. Oceanographers responded to data regarding the sea-floor. Seismologists entered the scene after geophysicists and oceanographers had collaborated to produce a sufficiently precise model of sea-floor spreading that seismological differences were expected. At this point, seismologists developed precise models of plate motions, plate tectonics. Once plate tectonics was developed in a precise way, continental geologists and other specialists in geosciences integrated the whole approach (plate tectonics and attendant views) and accepted it. There's a *subdisciplinary* pattern to the acceptance of mobilism.[18]

---

[18]Solomon [Sol01] was the first philosopher to observe this subdisciplinary pattern explicitly. Historical sources she cites corroborate her view, though they seem to prefer the view that evidential superiority ruled the day for mobilism; Solomon's own account includes the influence of consider-

Before turning to my diagnosis of this subdisciplinary pattern, I want to dispel two rival accounts of why it occurs. The first rival says that authority determines the decisions of scientific communities to accept or reject mobilism. On this view, scientific communities have an authority structure and certain individuals are regarded as authorities. Typically, they are established "names" in the field that the community regards as an expert on certain subjects. The approval or disapproval of authorities determines whether scientists accept or reject a proposal.

There is some reason to suppose that the authority view is correct. First, Stewart [Ste90] shows that the single best predictor that a scientist would resist mobilism is the number of articles he or she published. Second, many geoscientists report that resistance among eminent geoscientists slowed acceptance of mobilism. Nevertheless, the authority explanation is not very convincing. The notion of authority is pretty vague and appeals to it seem somewhat *ad hoc*. Patrick Blackett was among the most esteemed British scientists of his day, was the recipient of the 1947 Nobel Prize in physics, and in 1954, he and associated researchers published an article arguing for mobilism. If Blackett says "It looks to me like the continents move" it would seem on the authority view that a lot of minds should have changed as a result. Likewise, Keith Runcorn (another paleomagneticist) was a student of Harrold Jeffreys, who opposed mobilism well into the 1970s. Shouldn't we find Jeffreys influencing Runcorn, on the authority view? But Jeffreys' authority didn't determine Runcorn's attitudes and Blackett's authority didn't persuade geoscientists outside geophysics.

The authority view is vague, and that seems to invite *ad hoc* accounts of authority. This is a problem with the authority view, but it isn't the deepest one. There are two significant problems with the authority explanation. First, while one can

---

ations that philosophers of science have typically regarded as non-evidential. Solomon also sees the debates as occurring between three different hypotheses, stabilism, contractionism, and drift; I concur with Giere that contractionism and drift were largely independent hypotheses, and that it is most accurate to see the development of mobilism, which Solomon calls "drift", as rivaled by anti-mobilists who sometimes endorsed contractionist hypotheses.

cite particular cases of the influence of authority, authority itself doesn't explain the particular pattern of subdisciplinary acceptance we find: in each case, we have an alleged explanation (the authorities of the subdiscipline commend mobilist views), the explanation does not explain why we find the shift *among the authorities*. Second, many scientists violate the alleged authority structure. While some scientists, such as Blackett, were themselves authorities with license to do so, most, including Wegener, Wilson, and Runcorn, were not. Consequently, the authority view seems unappealing.[19]

The second rival to my own account says that information transfer among scientists was limited to members of subdisciplines; disciplines of geoscience remained sufficiently isolated from one another that one subdiscipline would remain unaware of the evidence in the possession of another subdiscipline. Geophysicsts, for example, discover lots of persuasive evidence of mobilism in the 50's but, since only geophysicists read geophysical literature, most of the rest of geoscientists remain unaware of geophysical results. Hence, while those arguments are persuasive and the evidence is good, too few geoscientists know about geophysics to influence the community's agreement. *Mutatis mutandis*, some story more of less like this is going to be told about the arguments and evidence that scientists offered, and that, it is supposed, accounts for the subdisciplinary pattern that we see.

This information isolation view is at odds with the historical record. While disciplinary boundaries do influence the dissemination of information, they're permeable barriers. Geoscientists were familiar with work outside their own specialty. Non-paleomagneticists, for example, responded to the research of Blackett and Runcorn, so they must at least have been aware of the ideas. Moreover, some of the seminal works related to mobilism were published in high-profile journals; Vine, Matthews and Wilson published their results that so influenced oceanographers in *Science* and

---

[19] Below I shall have something to say about the two motivations for accepting the authority view offered above.

Nature; nevertheless, those publications did not convert geoscientists outside oceanography. Mobilist papers published in *Nature* were certainly noticed in the community of geoscientists. So awareness of these results, and lack thereof, doesn't explain the subdisciplinary pattern. Furthermore, if the information isolation view were correct, one would expect that those scientists who did communicate across subdisciplinary lines would accept drift on the basis of the evidence held by those outside their field. This did not happen. It is, moreover, significant that even when scientists are aware of results outside their own discipline, those results have little or no persuasive force.

Agreement surrounding mobilism develops between the late 1950s and early 1970s. By 1970, agreement was nearly complete.[20] Many philosophers of science have diagnosed this shift as the result of overwhelming evidence on behalf of drift.[21] However, agreement was not achieved because individual scientists were sensitive to all these facts. Indeed, many scientists were aware of but insensitive to most of the facts. Personal or subdisciplinary factors, not widely available and shared evidential assessments, drove the agreement in geosciences. Indeed, it seems that the driving feature of agreement regarding plate tectonics and related ideas is disciplinary relevance. Agreement occurs one subdiscipline of geological science at a time (cf. [Sol01]). Where we find scientists whose acceptance does not follow the pattern of their subdiscipline, there are usually features of the ideas that had particular research relevance for them. The pattern of data for southern hemisphere geologists, for example, makes the explanatory power of the drift hypothesis especially persuasive; for other geologists, it

---

[20]One commonly finds 1965 or 1966 as the year in which the revolution occurred. This is, I think, incorrect. 1965 saw established agreement among specialists about formation of sea-floor ridges and their preferred account account of its cause, viz., sea-floor spreading. But to call this the moment at which the revolution completed would seem to me as mistaken as assigning Kepler to the completion of helio-centrism. Newton, of course, is the figure associated with the closure of that revolution. Without Newton, the door would have remained open for debate about the mechanism of planetary motions, and the debate would have continued. Plate tectonics, which is more than continental drift, was an essential element of the drift story. Those who date the geoscience revolution to 1965 or 66 neglect the importance this research had. (Apologies for the present historical over-simplifications regarding the scientific revolution. I hope the analogy is clear enough despite them.)

[21]See, for example, Giere[Gie88] and Laudan and Laudan [LL89].

is after plate tectonics provides precise predictions that influence their research that they come to take mobilism (and the related package of ideas) seriously. Oceanographers accept mobilism sometime before geologists, largely on the basis of its ability to handle data regarding faults in the ocean floor. In general, individual scientists come to accept representations as accurate only when those representations produce success in that scientist's research. A subdiscipline of a science reaches agreement only when, for reasons parochial to that subdiscipline, a representation has been successful for them.

In light of the foregoing discussion, the following generalization of scientific judgments suggests itself: scientists accept a representation as accurate only when that representation produces success in their research. Agreement within subdisciplines changes only when some scientists give mobilism an important role in thinking about some part of the discipline's subject matter. However, most scientific results are of the sort that Kuhn called "normal" and play no role in most of the thinking of most of the scientists in the relevant domain. But the principle that scientists accept only what's relevant to their research rules out their accepting any of that. However, a subtle modification to the present principle does the required work: scientists accept a representation as accurate only when it produces success in their research, or when their research and education disposes them to accept that the representation is accurate.[22]

This discussion will raise the question "what exactly is success?" But the answer here is that success varies from scientist to scientist and nothing precise can be said about what success is except the satisfaction (or appearance thereof) of scientists' goals according to their individual criteria of satisfaction.[23] Different scientists have

---

[22]That dispositions must be a part of an account of acceptance is antecedently motivated by considerations discussed in §1.1.

[23]Appearance thereof is a necessary caveat, for many of the goals of scientists will involve something at best indirectly accessible, such as accurate representation or explanation (and attendant acceptable representations that explain.) While truth or accuracy might be a goal, we can often only infer truth or accuracy by fallible means.

different goals. They have, moreover, different standards for assessing when their goals have been achieved. Because scientific judgments are typically theory-laden, scientists' beliefs about the subject domain itself will have a role in assessments of representations.[24] All scientists have some idiosyncratic beliefs, and those beliefs sometimes influence their judgments.

This is near the heart of the convergence model of scientific development: there is no one thing that constitutes scientific success, but rather a variety of standards of success, a variety of plans for achieving those standards, and a variety of ways to assess whether success has been achieved.

However, the philosophical attempts to find a standard of scientific success have not been entirely misguided; there have been many proposals about the appropriate standards of acceptance in scientific communities. I think that they have successfully cataloged some of the standards that scientists, as a matter of descriptive fact, have employed. Laudan [Lau84, 33-34] offers the following catalog of ways in which scientists assess theories, all of which have been endorsed by some philosophers:

> one scientist, for instance, may believe (with Popper) that a theory must make surprising, even startling, predictions, which turn out to be correct, before it is reasonable to accept it. Another may be willing to accept a hypothesis so long as it explains a broad range of phenomena, even if it has not made startling predictions. A third may say (with Nagel) that no theory is worth its salt until it has been tested against a wide variety of different kinds of supporting instances. A fourth may believe that a very large number of confirmations is probatively significant, regardless of the variety they exhibit. A fifth may demand that there be some direct and independent evidence for the existence of the entities postulated by

---

[24]'Theory-laden judgment' has meant many things in the philosophy of science literature. What *I* mean by it is a judgment whose psychological cause includes theoretical commitments of the scientist. I leave open whether that means that the content of the judgment is itself theoretical.

a hypothesis before it can reasonably be accepted.[25]

We may add to this list eliminative induction: a hypothesis may be accepted because, from among some range of exhaustive or probably exhaustive hypotheses, all alternatives have been eliminated besides one. All these are schematic presentations that raise questions about the details. For present purposes, it is sufficient to note that even at a fairly unrefined structural level, there are difference in how scientists reason.

Indeed, scientific acceptance need not happen as directly as the above suggests. Sometimes scientists will directly confront hypotheses with evidence and deploy a standard of assessment which, given their evidence, will rule for or against the hypothesis. On other occasions, scientific acceptance is indirect: scientists use a representation in their research for some purpose indirectly related to the representation itself, but, having succeeded in the research while using the representation in question, the scientist accepts the representation as accurate. (It is tempting to describe such cases as follows: a scientists accepts a representation provisionally as part of her research; the representation receives indirect reinforcement, similar to holistic testing. This reinforcement removes the provisional status of acceptance.) For example, the acceptance of plate tectonic models among geologists was not a result of testing such models directly, but instead the result of fruitful integration of plate tectonic models with the research projects of geologists, such as explanations of exotic terranes. While these models offered predictions and thus might be thought to have confronted direct geological evidence thereby, *predictions* of drift hypotheses and plate tectonics were available before geologists accepted either. The integration of those predictions yielded the acceptance of plate tectonics among geologists.

---

[25]As a historical point, I disagree with Laudan's suggestion that Popper thinks it's reasonable to accept theories (or even all their observational consequences) in the sense of accepting them as true. Nevertheless, Popper's constraint on scientific pursuit that theories should have startling novel predictions that are confirmed has been adopted as a constraint on scientific acceptance. The present passage from Laudan was not in a context where that distinction is particularly important and should not be read to suggest that Laudan thus misunderstands Popper.

2.3 Scientific Progress and the Merits of Diversity

To understand the merits of cognitive diversity in scientific communities, it is helpful to distinguish two broad domains of scientific development in which it has an effect: discovery and certification. Discovery involves introducing novelty in science; new techniques, representations, methods, and entities are all types of discovery. Certification involves processes that track accuracy; a process is certifying if, given a pair of rival representations, it selects the more accurate one. The notion of selection is obviously vague, but in the case of scientific processes, the matter is about how community agreement forms; selection is simply a matter of forming agreement. A pair of representations are rivals exactly if accepting one as it is typically used precludes accepting the other as it is typically used. (Note that this means that a representation with no use is not a rival of any other representation and is consequently not a subject for selection.)

The division between discovery and certification is closely related to the traditional one of discovery and justification. However, I reserve the term 'justification' for inquiry into the difference between knowledge and mere true belief. Moreover, the notion of justification is closely related to both reliability and rationality; the notion I am concerned with in the present discussion is specifically the capacity of scientific communities to form agreements about representations when and only when they are more accurate than available alternatives. Certification is very near to reliability as it is often conceived in epistemology. (Discussions of justification, rationality, and reliability are a prominent topic of chapter 5, where I discuss the place of knowledge in understanding science and scientific progress.)

Because of its similarity to the distinction between discovery and justification, I should mention that I do not intend that there are two different contexts in which scientists or scientific communities operate, nor do I intended that there are two different types of processes (processes for discovery and processes for certification.)

Rather, we have a conceptual distinction between discovering and certifying, and some science is more a matter of certification, while other science is more a matter of discovery. Nevertheless, diversity contributes to each, and the distinction helps us be clear about the contributions of diversity within science. Our antecedent concept of discovery includes at least some element of truth, reliability or certification because what counts as a discovery is something that is ultimately accepted by a scientific community. (Rötngen's X-rays were a discovery, Blondlot's N-Rays were not, but each was novel in its time.) Indeed, I think it is important that certification and discovery are inseparable within the developmental process of science; contribution of diversity to one is thus contribution of diversity to the other. (I discuss the reasons for this inseparability below.)

2.3.1 Computational Results Favoring Diversity

Social scientists Lu Hong and Scott Page [HP04] have developed an abstract model of group problem solving, and demonstrate that a group of randomly selected problem solvers out-performs the group of highest-ability problem solvers from the same population. Within their model, each problem solver is given a representation of problems, a "perspective," and strategies for locating a solution, a "heuristic." Given a space of solutions the agents search and valuations of the solutions in the space, agents' ability can be assessed by looking at the value of the solutions that they can find within the space; agents can thus be ranked by their ability. To model group problem solving, one allows agents to share solutions and work from shared solutions (which individual agents may be unable to find themselves) to find further solutions. Hong and Page's remarkable result, for one particular implementation of this model, is that randomly selected groups of diverse agents out-perform a selection of the best agents.

Thus abstractly described, it may be difficult to see how Hong and Page can establish their result, so it is helpful to provide more precise details about their particular implementation of this model. What they imagine is that agents look for solutions for a collection of n points organized on a circle; each point is assigned a random value from the uniform distribution in the interval $[0, 100]$, and agents' task is to find the largest value on the circle that she can. Each agent's heuristic allows her to check certain points to the right of her current position on the circle. If one of those points has a greater value, the agent moves to that point and performs the search again. The procedure continues until the agent is unable to locate a better solution. The value of the agent's final solution will depend on her starting position on the circle; her ability can be measured by looking at the average value of her solution given each starting point on the circle.[26] For example, an agent may have the heuristic (1,5,7) and be given the starting point 87 on a circle of 100 points. She searches point 88 (87 + 1); if point 88 has a higher value than point 87, she searches point 93 (88 + 5), else she searches 92 (87 + 5). Suppose 88 has a higher value, then she searches from point 93 to whether 100 (93 + 7) has a higher value than 93. If so, she searches point 1 (101 - 100, we're back at the start of the circle), and if not, she searches point 94 (93 + 1). She keeps searching until none of her three searches finds a point to the right with a higher value. The mean value of her solution from all possible starting points evaluates her ability.

To model group problem solving, agents sequentially develop problem solutions and pass their solution to the next agent in the sequence. If that agent finds a better solution, that solution is given to the next agent in the sequence, otherwise, the previous solution is passed on. Once the final agent has attempted the problem, the first agent begins with the final agents' solution. This repeats until every agent seeks a solution but finds no new superior solution. Once again, collective performance is

---

[26]Let ϕ denote the agent's heuristic, $\phi(x)$ denote the stopping point when given x as a starting point, and $V(x)$ the function that gives the value of the solution at point x, then, for n starting positions, the ability of the agent is $\frac{1}{n}\sum_{i=1}^{n} V(\phi(i))$.

measured by taking the mean value of the solution for each possible starting point in the solution space. In order to have a definite population of agents to work with, Hong and Page allow every heuristic that searches a number k of positions no more than l points from the starting position. Hence, they consider each heuristic, ϕ, of the form $(\phi_1, \phi_2, \ldots \phi_k)$ for $\phi_i \in \{1, 2, \ldots l\}$.

Hong and Page report the result of a representative run of their computational experiment:

> The best agent scored 87.3; the worst agent scored 84.3; the average score of the 10 best agents was 87.1, and the average score of the 10 randomly selected agents was 85.6. The collective performance of the 10 best agents had a value of 93.2; their average diversity (averaged over all possible pairs) was 0.72. The collective performance of the 10 randomly selected agents was 94.7; their average diversity was 0.92. [HP04, 16387]

The difference in performance between a random group and a high ability group is 1.5; the difference between the average of agents in the first group and the average of agents in the second group is -1.6. The magnitude of the difference between the diverse and high-ability groups is the same as that between a typical high-ability problem solver and the ordinary problem solver. Diversity makes a significant difference.

So far as I can tell, the reason diverse groups of agents in Hong's and Page's model are more successful is that diverse groups search a greater proportion of the solution space than less diverse ones. As they define diversity, it may simply be constitutive of diverse groups that they do so. This does not undermine their conclusion, but one might ask whether real-world cognitive diversity increases the search space that groups have available to them. If not, then Hong's and Page's conclusion depends on a false substantive assumption that diversity increases a group's ability to search a solution space.

From the perspective of the present work, what Hong and Page seem to show is something about discovery. The differences among agents have to do with their ability to find solutions to problems, but all agents share evaluations of problem solutions, there is no problem of disagreement among them, and their evaluations of solutions exactly match the solutions' values. What is the explanation for this result? The answer is that the ten best agents have highly similar heuristics and tend, as a result, to offer only similar problem solutions. The explanation, as Hong and Page put it, is that the high ability agents tend to become stuck on a local maximum because of their similarity. Precisely because lower ability agents search the space differently, the group is able to consider a greater number of potential solutions and thus able to find better ones. In short, diversity promotes discovery.

This computational proof supports judgments regarding diversity that philosophers have made. Diversity has been supposed to let a thousand flowers bloom. Also, diversity has been alleged to promote better divisions of labor within the scientific community. In each of these cases, philosophers argue that diversity increases the available material that scientists have to work with. In the latter case, it is further thought that, given that any research project in science has a non-negligible chance of failure, it is better not to have all of our eggs in one basket, so to speak. Kitcher [Kit93, chapter 8] is representative of this latter idea, and develops it in a number of more precise and interesting ways.

There are problems with analogizing science with Hong and Page's model of group problem solving: the value of solutions in the space is uniformly distributed, but it seems like even modestly valuable problem solutions in science are exceptional. I have already mentioned the issue of a potentially false and substantive assumption that diverse groups search a larger space of solutions than uniform ones. However, as we recall the notion of a perspective as I have defined it (cf. Hong and Page's definition within their model), this seems like a highly plausible assumption.

Philosophers Michael Weisberg and Ryan Muldoon [WM09] have recently generated computer models of division of cognitive labor that further the view that diversity promotes successful science. They model scientists and collections of scientists by imagining them as agents in a *epistemic landscape*, which is a multidimensional space that represents research approaches and solutions or results that research approaches yield. Of course, a landscape may have many or few dimensions, depending on how many facets of research approaches one wishes to consider.[27] In the [WM09], they use a three dimensional space, with x and y coordinates representing arbitrary elements of research approaches and z coordinates representing significant truth. Each coordinate pair is mapped to a single value in the z dimension, thus representing the significant truth discovered by that research approach, with greater values of z representing greater significance. Within their landscape metaphor, elevation represents significance. For their computer model, Weisberg and Muldoon use a pair of Gausian functions to determine the elevation of the landscape in two regions of epistemic significance, thereby generating two "hills" where productive research may occur. (To simplify the mathematics of the model, they use a discrete grid of 101 by 101 "patches" representing two components of a research approach.)

Weisberg and Muldoon model individual scientists by giving them rules for navigating their landscape; moving around the landscape involves taking different research approaches and, thereby, producing different results. Different rules yield different behavior for agents. The rules that they investigate have scientists evaluate their movement based on their assessments of significance, i.e., by checking altitude.[28] One simple rule is a hill climbing rule that (to leave out some small details) has agents move in one direction as long as they find continual increases in significance, but if significance drops, they go back a step and randomly change directions. Given enough

---

[27] Epistemic landscapes are clearly intended to be flexible representational tools that could include nearly any factor influencing scientific decisions as a dimension. They list four elements that they take ordinarily to be a part of a research approach: research questions being investigated; instruments and techniques used to gather data; methods used to analyze data; and background theories used to interpret data [WM09, 228].

[28] Weisberg and Muldoon assume a uniform assessment of significance within their model; they do not, however, make any special claims about what significance is. Obviously, I disagree that scientists typically share assessments of significance.

time, agents with this rule always find a local maximum. These agents are completely oblivious to all past results except their most recently explored patch.

Scientists aware of results their discipline has produced can be modeled by giving them rules that are sensitive to whether a patch has already been explored. In Weisberg and Muldoon's model, they give agents rules that allow them to search the Moore neighborhood (the eight adjacent patches) of their current patch and decide how to proceed based on their information about their Moore neighborhood. One such rule they call the "follow rule":

> Ask: Have any of the approaches in my Moore neighborhood been investigated?
>
> If yes: Ask: Is the significance of any of the investigated approaches greater than the significance of my current approach?
>
> If yes: Move towards the approach of greater significance. If there is a tie, pick randomly between them.
>
> If no: If there is an unvisited approach in the Moore neighborhood, move to it, otherwise, stop.
>
> If no: Choose a new approach in the Moore neighborhood at random.

Here, significance is decisive in the decision making procedures of scientists.[29] This particular rule is, unsurprisingly, not very effective at discovering significant regions of the landscape because the agents tend to explore areas that have already been explored. Indeed, Followers are slightly less successful than agents with a simple hill climbing rule, as measured by the number of patches with non-zero significance that the group explores. The success of the group generally reflects the number of agents in the group; larger groups out-perform smaller ones.

Another rule, and a far more effective one, that they investigate that call "Maverick":

---

[29] This (as Weisberg and Muldoon acknowledge) assumes that there are no costs to changing research approach, and so obviously includes some idealization.

Maverick Rule: Ask: Is my current approach yielding equal or greater significance than my previous approach?

If yes: Ask: Are any of the patches in my Moore neighborhood unvisited?

If yes: Move towards the unvisited patch. If there are multiple unvisited patches, pick randomly between them.

If no: If any of the patches in my neighborhood have a higher significance value, go towards one of them, otherwise stop.

If no: Go back 1 patch and set a new random heading.

Mavericks only repeat research when either they have no choice or the current patch seems to be on a decreasingly significant path. Mavericks far out perform both Hill Climbers and Followers. A group of Mavericks nearly always finds both local maxima.

Weisberg and Muldoon also consider mixed groups of followers and mavericks. Introducing ten mavericks to larger group of followers considerably improves the performance of the group. This is not merely because the group receives the individual research of mavericks; following mavericks is better than following followers, and consequently, adding mavericks to a group of followers makes some followers more effective. This complements my thesis, for it shows that mixed groups profit from diversity. However, one might suspect the particular results that they offer also suggest that diversity is less important than individual effectiveness. Although mixed groups of followers and mavericks outperform pure groups of followers, and although in such mixed groups the improved performance is greater than the added marginal performance of the mavericks, the success of mixed groups is directly correlated with the proportion of mavericks in the group. The situation is one of diminishing returns: increases in the follower to maverick ratio are beneficial to the degree that ratio is closer to zero.

However, this important objection is not what Weisberg and Muldoon show. The kind of diversity they consider is a diversity of search algorithms. The kind of diversity that I consider is a diversity of perspectives. Within their model, a perspective is really much more like a research approach than a search rule. For good reason (see fn. 27), research approaches may include any number of factors, but they carefully note that prominent factors in research approaches include research questions being investigated, instruments and techniques used to gather data, methods used to analyze data, and background theories used to interpret data [WM09, 228]. Within my own framework, the follower rule is one that says (effectively) "employ perspectives of others, with a preference for perspectives that have succeeded", while the Maverick rule says "employ perspectives no one else has, with a preference for successful perspectives when no novel perspective is available." Consequently, the Maverick rule is really a rule that prefers diversity while the follower rule is one that encourages uniformity. Weisberg and Muldoon's results complement my own thesis nicely.

Weisberg and Muldoon's results principally relate to issues of discovery. Their measure of success, "epistemic progress", is simply a function of how much significant research scientists do; no question of certification ever arises within their landscapes.

There are some considerable objections to the structure of epistemic landscapes that Weisberg and Muldoon use, and while their results complement my thesis, the limitations of their models should also be recognized. I would share with objectors some concerns about epistemic landscapes.[30] The most general way to state my first concern is that approaches used to model epistemic problems must make substantive assumptions about the nature of the solution space. In particular, there are few local maxima in the solution spaces they consider; because they choose Gaussian functions to map elevations onto research approaches, and have only two regions of significance, any straight path in the space of approaches has at most two local maxima. Why? This assumes that adjacent research approaches have similar prospects for signifi-

---

[30]To my knowledge, these criticisms are original to me. Written correspondence with Weisberg and Muldoon did not indicate that these concerns had been expressed by others. Hence, I *would* share these concerns with objectors because these objectors are hypothetical.

cance. Indeed, it's unclear what makes a particular choice ordering on an axis in the space of the topic, i.e., what should ultimately make patches adjacent?[31] Consider the following toy topic involving researchers experimenting with pairings of three drugs from one group (group X) with three drugs from a second group (group Y) in order to see which combination achieves the best health outcome. Clearly there are nine combinations of drugs to consider, and each combination will have some outcome, an elevation from the topic space of X,Y. But the topography of the solution space (the elevations) depends on which drug in X we call 1 and which drug in Y we call 1, and there's no reason to order the drugs in any way antecedently. This in itself presents no problem, but once we combine it with search rules that make explicit reference to the Moore neighborhood of an agent, the choice becomes very significant—the results our model produces just is a function (given some search algorithm) of the choice of orderings in X and Y.

Weisberg and Muldoon claim that "approaches likely to yield significant results cluster together, and are not scattered randomly through the epistemic landscape," but, as the present toy example shows, it is unclear what distance means in a topic space, so it's unclear why they are entitled to assume anything about clustering. Moreover, what seems relevant, given the use of proximity in search rules, is how scientists search the space of research approaches, which may be totally independent of natural ways of ordering dimensions in the topic space. For example, if drugs x_1 and x_2 (but not x_3) have a certain physiological effect, then making them adjacent to one another may seem natural; however, if that fact is not suspected by the scientists involved in the research, then it probably won't influence the way they search the space of research options. This suggests a further, related problem: the topography of a landscape may be relative to agents (e.g., if they have different appraisals of

---

[31]Ryan Muldoon pointed out to me that this becomes even more problematic when we consider agents with different accounts of significance; in such a case, each agent's axes have a different ordering.

significance).

This problem is important. Consider black-body radiation, the photoelectric effect, and Bohr's solar system model of the atom: these problems share that they are the first three significant uses of Planck's quantization procedure in physics. The latter two borrowed that procedure from the initial one, but Bohr's and Einstien's problems themselves seem to have very little in common (at least, antecedently, from the perspective of the scientists working on them.) The fact that the problems have little in common inclines me to say that in the topic space (X,Y), they should be distant from one another, but then Einstein and Bohr need search algorithms that search space outside their Moore neighborhood, if we want to represent them as "borrowing" Planck's procedure. Perhaps this particular example is inappropriate to treatment by landscapes, but I think nevertheless that the initial problem of the relation between search rules and topography remains. In fairness to Weisberg and Muldoon, I should mention that they don't intend epistemic landscapes to be good models of whole sciences, but only relatively localized topics of investigation that one might think of as normal science. Hence, the present criticism really applies only insofar as one attempts to generalize their claims beyond the realm where they intend them to inform our understanding.

Assumptions about solution spaces are typically extremely difficult to justify—they may even be unjustifiable—because solution spaces of different problems often lack similarities. Even if we had an antecedent means of specifying an ordering for each dimension of the research approaches, there is no guarantee (that I can see) that the solution space will have many or few local maxima, and whether those maxima will tend to cluster or be uniformly distributed through the problem space. But if this is correct, it is likely that there are no rules for dividing cognitive labor, since the topography of the solution space will have a determining effect on which distribution of Mavericks and Followers (or whatever rules you choose) will be optimal.[32]

---

[32]Ryan Muldoon implicated in written correspondence that the "No Free Lunch Theorem" says

Perhaps we can generate interesting results to the effect that the relative proportion of Mavericks and Followers appropriate to a problem space is a function of the number of local maxima in the space, but that doesn't tell us anything about divisions of cognitive labor *generally*, since we don't know generally what problem spaces are like. (Such a point may also be leveled against models of division of cognitive labor, such as Kitcher's, that rely on rewards correlated to marginal contributions, since, in those models, optimal distributions of labor are achieved because scientists correctly can estimate their probability of marginal contribution.) Moreover, it may be that other rules are better suited to problem spaces with many local maxima.

My second concern is that Weisberg and Muldoon map research approaches into the solution space one-one rather than a one-many or many-many. It seems most likely that, for many topics of research, there are many research approaches that might yield a given significant truth as a result, and most research approaches (for a given topic) will yield more than one significant result. Of course, scientists often publish their results one at a time, but successful research groups tend to generate many publications in their topic area, and a related research approach often underlies their papers.[33]

The assumption of one-one mapping is also problematic because results are only typically significant the first time. Consequently, if approaches A and B have, respectively, $\{x, y\}$ and $\{y, z\}$ as the truths each reveals, then A is more significant before B has been explored because of the overlap regarding y.

---

there exists an epistemic landscape in which the Followers outperform Mavericks.

[33] An important point that Weisberg and Muldoon raise is that many scientific research topics are of a sort where comprehensiveness is at least as important as finding the most significant results; within the metaphor of a landscape, exploring large regions of it may be more important than reaching the points of highest altitude. Many scientific topics seems to share some structure with topics like those exactly analogous to the topics for which Muldoon and Weisberg develop landscapes and some structure with topics emphasized by Kitcher, who typically models scientific communities with a question that has a fairly specific correct answer. I should note that it seems possible to construct landscapes that emphasize the different structure of the topics; a plateau topography suggests many important results of similar value, while a mountain peak topography suggests a single important result.

A final problem with Weisberg and Muldoon's landscapes approach occurs to me: the significance of scientific results is sometimes dependent on what else we truly believe. x and z may be independently insignificant results even though x-and-z is a quite significant result. In this situation, exploring A becomes more significant once B has been explored, and vice versa.

These final two points seem to reveal a path dependence of significance, but they may also involve technical problems that arise from associating patches with more than one truth. Nevertheless, it is difficult for me to see how to avoid associating some research approaches with more than one significant result. As I have already mentioned, the key for Weisberg and Muldoon is to restrict their model to topics of "normal science". Within this dissertation it is important not to extend their result too generally. However, in several respects, the metaphor of epistemic landscapes suggests that cognitive diversity is generally profitable. As we envision the various possible topographies of epistemic landscapes, it seems clear that no one search algorithm will be appropriate to them all. Moreover, it's clear that no one type of landscape would be appropriate to scientific problems in general.

2.3.2 Inseparability of Discovery and Certification

The foregoing discussion of the merits of diversity have all emphasized ways in which diversity increases the power of scientific communities to make discoveries. In the Hong and Page results, we see that diversity improves the capacity of scientific communities to search the space of problem solutions. Weisberg and Muldoon also reveal a role for diversity in discovery. But none of this says anything about the role of diversity in certification. My view is that agreement in scientific communities is a certifying process because of features which the agreement process possesses. Those features arise in large part because of diversity. In the remainder of this chapter, I discuss the relationship between diversity and certification, as well as a first reason to think that scientific communities as whole are apt to select accurate representations in their agreements. In the next chapter, I extend the discussion of certification by considering the role of diversity in realizing an explanatory defense of realism.

Thomas Kuhn's view in *Structure of Scientific Revolutions* [Kuh70] was criticized for making scientific theory choice a mere matter of mob psychology. In "Objectivity, Value Judgment and Theory Choice", Kuhn responded by articulating more carefully an account of theory choice that he believed sustained the rationality of theory choice while accommodating the history of science in which he saw no algorithmic rules. Kuhn thus attempted to situate himself between traditional rationalism and the thorough anti-rationalism sometimes attributed to *Structure*. Traditional rationalism attempted to provide algorithmic rules of theory choice to science and explain scientific success with the power of those rules. Kuhn rejects this picture in [Kuh77], and claims that instead, scientists share a set of "values"—accuracy, consistency, breadth, simplicity, and fecundity—that they employ in theory choice. However, these values are not rules for theory choice. They receive different weighting and different interpretation from different scientists. According to Kuhn, this allows the possibility of disagreement among scientists, while sustaining rationality, at least in the sense of making scientific decisions a matter of more than "mob psychology" or mere political preference. The values of accuracy, consistency and so forth have genuine epistemic force.

Such a position naturally raises the question 'are there correct weightings and best interpretations of the values?'. Kuhn answers 'no'. Instead, scientific development requires a plurality of interpretations and weightings of scientific values:

> ...[M]uch work, both theoretical and experimental, is ordinarily required before a new theory can display sufficient accuracy and scope to generate widespread conviction. In short, before the group accepts it, a new theory has been tested over time by the research of a number of men, some

working within it, others within its traditional rival. Such a mode of development, however, *requires* a decision process which permits rational men to disagree, and such disagreement would be barred by the shared algorithm which philosophers have generally sought. If it were at hand, all conforming scientists would make the same decision at the same time. With standards for acceptance set too low, they would move from one attractive global viewpoint to another, never giving traditional theory an opportunity to supply equivalent attractions. With standards set higher, no one satisfying the criterion of rationality would be inclined to try out the new theory, to articulate it in ways which showed its fruitfulness or displayed its accuracy and scope. [Kuh77, 112]

In this view, Kuhn is one of the first writers to recognize, implicitly, the inseparability of discovery and certification. To achieve acceptance within the scientific community, scientific work typically requires refinement in response to early detractors; such refinements are instances of scientific discovery, but they are also essential to changing community attitudes toward the scientific work in question. Kuhn is noting a role for division of cognitive labor, as have many recent writers. However, most recent writers have focused on the role of division of cognitive labor in making science efficient; Kuhn's emphasis is upon an essential role for divisions within a community that certifies scientific results.

His discussion in "Objectivity, Value Judgment and Theory Choice" [Kuh77] has not received enough credit for shaping contemporary thought in the philosophy of science; this, I suspect, is because that essay has typically been seen as backing off or clarifying the position of *The Structure of Scientific Revolutions*. Moreover, [Kuh77] has typically been examined for the particulars (or lack thereof) of theory choice in science that Kuhn discusses. As such, its important novel contributions are under-appreciated: it is the role of division of labor that underscores the point about diversity, not the account itself; indeed, the account itself can be abandoned while that role for divided labor is retained in another one.

According to Kuhn's account, without cognitive diversity, science cannot proceed in the way required for progress. Kuhn gets the necessary mode of scientific development wrong. What is necessary, and Kuhn gets this right, is allowing scientists to "try out... new theory, to articulate it in ways which showed its fruitfulness or displayed its accuracy and scope" while "giving traditional theory an opportunity to supply equivalent attractions." (Kuhn states the point in terms of *theory*, which is mistaken, but so long as we understand the point as applying to scientific research more generally, it is correct.) But, as is common in Kuhn's writing, he moves quickly from a correct account of what scientists must *do* to an account of what scientists must *accept*; that move is mistaken. Some kind of diversity is required, but, for all he has said, it is unclear that the kind he cites—diversity of modes of acceptance—is required.

There are two basic criticisms of Kuhn's position. First, it is alleged that scientists need only be able to pursue or investigate scientific options in order to achieve his requisite division of labor. Second, it is claimed that scientists only need to disagree about factual matters, not matters of value and method, in order to achieve it.

However, these responses to Kuhn do not undercut his more important point, because all that these responses establish is that Kuhn's particular mode of development is unnecessary for science to achieve its results. The first response says that scientific progress requires only values that allow scientists to *pursue* a theory in order for the necessary theoretical and experimental work to happen. If so, the option to pursue theories suffices for science to function, and the norms of *acceptance* can be uniform. The second argument claims that disagreement about weights and interpretations is unnecessary because variation in available information suffices to produce the required division of labor. However, while these arguments show that Kuhn's mode of development is not necessary, all that they establish is a counterfactual possibility;

as we saw in §2.2, Kuhn's mode of development is more nearly the one that science actually displays.

The view that scientific disagreement arises from variation in available information implies a scientific history of largely evidential debates; what history actually reveals is that scientific disagreement usually occasions both evidential and methodological debate. The informational variability account of scientific disagreement is at odds with empirical (historical) evidence. The informational account bears a close resemblance to one of the accounts of the sub-disciplinary pattern of acceptance in geoscience, discussed above, and many of those comments apply here as well. This objection to Kuhn's claim that variable values are *necessary* thus seems on point—for all Kuhn has said, informational variability seems sufficient. However, as a matter of fact, informational variability does not seem to exhaust the variety of diversity that science reveals. Moreover, the informational variability account concedes the point that is most important from the present standpoint: cognitive diversity is essential to scientific development.

Regarding the attempt to circumvent Kuhn's mode of development by appeal to the distinction between pursuit and acceptance, we have already discussed pursuit and acceptance (under another name) above: research relevance was seen to be critical to scientific acceptance when we discussed the revolution in geoscience. Research relevance itself involves pursuit and use of scientific representations. *Facts* of pursuit and facts of acceptance are consequently not readily separable. While one might maintain different views about the *norms* of pursuit and acceptance (viz., that they are separable), it's unclear what the point of such regularly violated norms is.

The importance of Kuhn's observation is not to be neglected. What Kuhn has shown is that discovery and certification are inseparable: in order for scientific research to display its merits, a social process of criticism and response is essential. In order to achieve that process, diversity is an essential element because it allows the community to make the discoveries needed for those merits to be displayed. Those merits are essentially evidential. Consequently, diversity contributes to the certification of scientific theories. In short: diversity promotes discovery, discovery promotes certification, and, therefore, diversity promotes certification.

CHAPTER 3

Explaining Progress

In the previous chapter, we assessed several features of agreement formation in science and discussed the ways in which features of scientific communities and the processes of scientific acceptance gave rise to a scientific community apt to produce important discoveries. This also led to an argument that the particular processes of agreement formation lead to well-certified science because discovery is essential to certification. Discovery and certification are inseparable, so what contributes to discovery contributes to certification. The diversity which contributed to discovery, therefore, also contributed to certification. However, such a process contributes to certification only inessentially: any alternative process that produced the requisite discoveries would produce the relevant certification. That does not mean that alternative processes are available to science, but it does mean that, insofar as it contributes to discovery, diversity contributes to scientific certification only indirectly.

In this chapter, I argue that the mere fact of convergence within communities that we identify as scientific certifies topics of their agreement. The argument of the present chapter has its roots in the explanatory defense of realism: I argue that convergent agreements require accuracy as an explanation. In chapter 2, we saw that amid diverse standards of acceptance, heterogeneous technical methods, varying research goals and differential access to evidence, and despite rivals that enjoy at least some successes for the community, scientific representations find uniform acceptance in the scientific community. And the explanation is not far away: scientific representations achieve uniform acceptance because they are more accurate than any available alternative. The present discussion will elucidate the relationship between my own view and traditional scientific realism. Because it bears a close similarity to the explanatory defense of realism, my argument is subject to objections following the pessimistic induction. In this chapter, I address the pessimistic induction and draw some conclusions about the explanatory defense of realism and my own version (roughly speaking) thereof.

3.1 The Explanatory Defense of Progress

J. J. C. Smart argued against instrumentalism that it requires commitment to cosmic coincidences. Cloud chambers and galvanometers behave in their characteristic ways but, according to instrumentalism, this is a sort of accident: insofar as they are caused to behave in any particular way, we have no special reason to think it is the causes our theories of these devices suggest. Given this and manifold other accidents, instrumentalism strains credulity. Consequently, we should accept realism instead of instrumentalism. This argument bears close similarity to the explanatory defense. Psillos [Psi99, 73] notes that Smart's argument is really a plausibility argument, not an explanatory defense, because it never appeals to an inference to the best explanation. Rather, Smart appeals to assessments of plausibility of realism and instrumentalism given the fact the world behaves as scientific theories predict.[1] Psillos highlights that the considerations that lead scientists to accept their theories are not the considerations that lead Smart to realism. Nevertheless, Smart's contention that alternatives to realism conjure residual mysteries has the spirit of a realist conviction that scientific success cries out for explanation.[2]

Grover Maxwell also offered a version of the explanatory defense of realism. Unlike Smart, Maxwell seems to think that distinctively scientific considerations motivate the realist inference. In particular, considerations of simplicity, coherence, and other

---

[1] Psillos further notes that Smart's overall attitude is that the argument for realism is part of a distinctively philosophical debate in which empirical test is impossible.

[2] Smart's version is also worth noting because plausibility assessments may play an important background role for realists: sympathies for realism may involve this alleged implausibility of anti-realist alternatives.

superempirical virtues play a role in the plausibility assessments that are part of the realist argument that scientific theories are probably true if they are successful. Consequently, though the particular considerations that motivate scientists to accept theories are not part of the realist argument, the considerations that Maxwell's realism employs are scientific. Scientists and Maxwell's realist share theoretical desiderata but not data.

Note a lacuna in Smart's and Maxwell's arguments: scientific realism is a thesis not only about the truth of scientific theories, but also about the merit of accepting them; realism says something about scientific theories qua scientific theory, not scientific theories qua successful theory. These arguments purport to establish something about instrumentally successful science, but they can't purport to establish an expectation of scientific success. Realism is not only a thesis about successful science, but a thesis about sciences: while the arguments thus far (attempt to) explain why successful sciences have succeeded, they don't explain why sciences produce instrumental success. It might be instructive to put the lacuna in terms of explanatory contrast classes. One question is "why has science succeeded rather than failed?" and realists answer "because it is true". Another question is "why has science been true rather than false?", but realists cannot plausibly answer this "because it is true". Both Maxwell and Smart offer a fledgling defense of realism that says it is successful because true. But a full-fledged defense of realism can argue that science succeeds because it is scientific.

An epistemic dimension of realism involves explaining why sciences produce truth and accuracy. Truth is the explanation of producing instrumental success, but what is the explanation of producing truth? It is this element of realism that has exercised realists like Boyd and Psillos. It also highlights why extra-scientific considerations for realism are incomplete considerations: to vindicate realism, it is not enough to show that according to extra-scientific considerations science has achieved success; one must further show that scientific considerations, i.e., factors operating within scientific communities, vindicate the realist attitude toward science. Without this, there is no reason to expect science to achieve truth and hence success.

Richard Boyd is most famously associated with the thread of realist thought that accounts for its reliable methods; as he puts it, "a realistic account of scientific theories is a component in the only scientifically plausible explanation for the instrumental reliability of scientific methodology" [Boy84, 58]. According to Boyd, all scientific judgment is deeply theory-laden; in particular, scientists rely on background theories to make judgment of projectibility and degree of confirmation. The reliability of those judgments can only be explained, according to Boyd, if we suppose that the theoretical claims that determine these judgments are approximately true.

Psillos offers an explanatory defense of realism similar to Boyd's. (He acknowledges a debt to Boyd in his defense.) Psillos [Psi99, 79] offers the following roles for theory in scientific judgment "[s]cientists use accepted background theories in order to form their expectations, to choose the relevant methods for theory-testing, to devise experimental set-ups, to calibrate instruments, to assess the experimental evidence, to choose among competing theories, [and] to assess newly suggested hypotheses...." Moreover, scientific predictions and experiments are successful. The best explanation of this success is that elements of background theories that assert "specific causal connections or mechanisms" that yield these predictions and experiments are approximately true.

The Boyd-Psillos defense does not vindicate scientific methods. It takes for granted the efficacy of scientific method and tries to explain that efficacy via truth of theory. Their point is that appeals to truth are necessary to understand why science reliably produces instrumental success. However, scientific methods themselves are within the picture, unlike the defenses of Smart and of Maxwell.

I have diagrammed the traditional (e.g., Boyd-Psillos) explanatory defense of realism in figure 3.1. To the right is my own view. The symmetries are obvious, the difference is that I replace consensus methodological practices with convergence.

(Each of the arrows in fig. 3.1 my be read as a relation with the arrow indicating the order of the relata.)

Convergence contributes to the certification of scientific representations because in order for a representation to achieve uniform acceptance it must be instrumentally successful. Since scientists accept representations only when they have some role in their research (see chapter 2, especially pp. 58–59) and scientific research is diverse, a representation must have a role in many scientific research projects before it will be uniformly accepted. If having a role in successful research is instrumental success (and it seems a fair definition), instrumental success is essential to community acceptance. In chapter 2, we cataloged several standards of scientific acceptance, many of which are the standard varieties philosophers of science have discussed. If we conjoin this with the realist contention that the best explanation of the instrumental success of science is that its representations are accurate, it follows that convergence begets accuracy. From the fact that scientific communities are diverse, it follows that science is likely accurate.

The conclusion of this argument must be mitigated. As stated, it concludes that diversity gives us accuracy. We must be careful of how we understand this claim. In chapter 1, I claimed that accuracy is often a relative rather than absolute notion: "r_1 is more accurate than r_2" is the principle form of accuracy assessments. Thus, it does not typically make sense to say "r is accurate" except as shorthand for some contextually determined relative assessment. In the present case, the issue is of a scientific agreement being more accurate than its rivals. So the claim here is that the best explanation of the instrumental success required for agreement to shift is the greater accuracy of the new agreement over any rival alternative, especially the past topic of agreement.

The conception of accuracy detailed in §1.3 and account of acceptance in chapter 2, though independently motivated, are connected. One may characterize scientific research as an attempt to answer questions about nature; accepting a representation

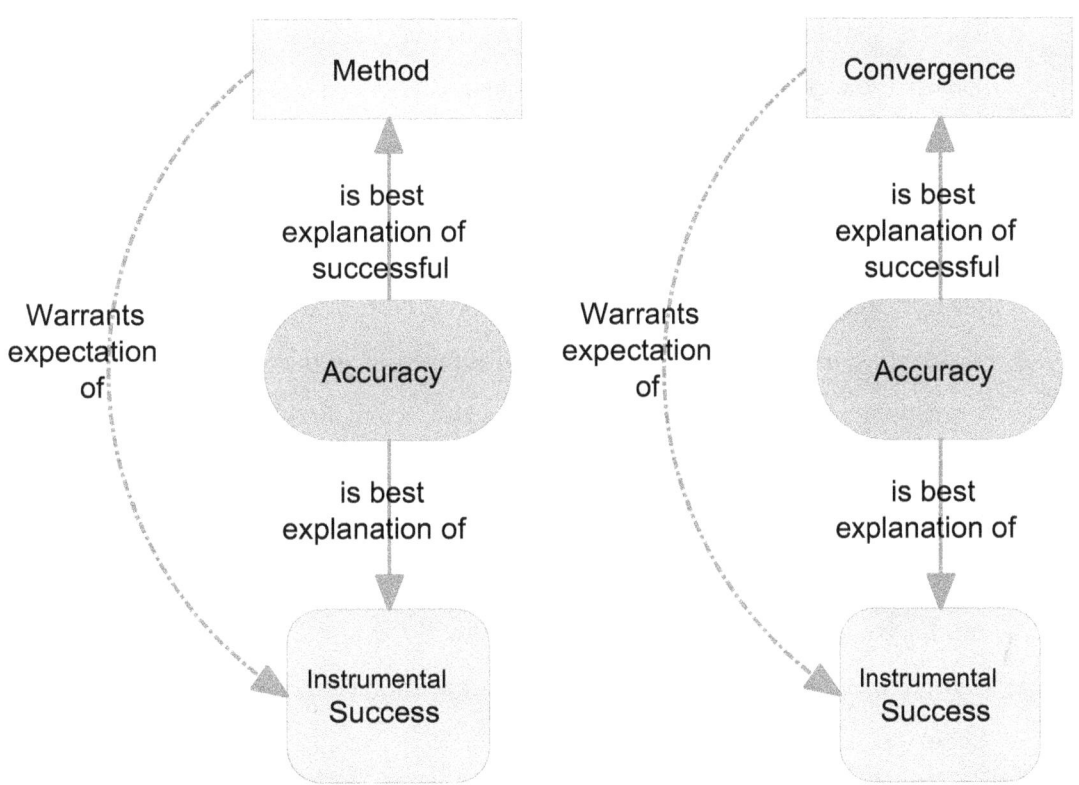

FIGURE 3.1. Convergence and the Explanatory Defense.

as accurate results from a representation's having a role in scientific research. This means that the representations facilitate answering questions. The model of accuracy presented earlier characterizes it in terms of the ability of representations to answer questions; r_1 is more accurate than r_2 iff r_1 truly answers questions better than r_2 does (where "better" is understood as expected utility.)

Boyd and Psillos don't correctly appreciate the degree to which background beliefs of scientists play a role in determining what methodological injunctions scientists will draw from a given theory; put more generally, Boyd and Psillos overstate the cognitive uniformity of scientists. In order for the Boyd-Psillos explanatory defense of the epistemic dimension of realism to succeed, theory must uniformly condition scientific responses to nature.[3] However, theory influences scientific judgment (method, and so forth) only as part of a whole that also includes auxiliary assumptions, technical approaches, and methodological commitments. Moreover, to attribute a whole to the scientific community ignores the diversity of scientific communities. This is a significant difference between Boyd and Psillos and me. Boyd and Psillos think shared theory uniformly conditions judgments of scientists. Theory is the primary influence upon scientific practice, and it excludes or over-rides idiosyncratic belief. We might summarize this by saying that according to Boyd and Psillos, theory dominates judgment. On my view, idiosyncratic factors are more important; idiosyncracies mediate "theory's" influence.[4]

As a result, the Boyd-Psillos explanatory defense of realism has a chimerical ex-

---

[3] Philosophical tendencies to speak of theories whenever we speak about scientific representations reveal their occasionally pernicious influence in the present context.

[4] Boyd and Psillos both seem implicitly committed to a version of Laudan's "covariance fallacy". It is the "fallacy" of assuming that various axiological, methodological and doxasitic differences among scientists covary, so that, for example, differences among scientists about whether p must occasion differences of a methodological sort. (These aren't Laudan's terms, but it is easier to put his assertions in the terms in which I accept them than in his terms with caveats about his terminology. His terms are 'axiological', 'methodological', and 'factual'. See [Lau84, 43–50] for his discussion of the "fallacy".) Laudan's fallacy, like other things occasionally dubbed fallacies by philosophers (I'm reminded of G. E. Moore's naturalistic fallacy) is not so much a fallacy as a bad assumption that often lurks as an undisclosed premise in an argument. The Boyd-Psillos version of the covariance fallacy could be summarized "science is uniformly theory laden."

planandum. They locate the methodological reliability of sciences in a uniform practice of scientists, but that uniform practice does not exist. If we seek an explanatory defense of realism, we must find something other than method that explains scientific reliability. As depicted in figure 3.1, I replace method with convergence.

3.2 Pessimistic Objections

Because I appeal to the instrumental success of science as requiring an explanation via accuracy to defend the view the science progresses toward greater accuracy, I must confront the challenges to realists' inferences presented by the pessimistic induction. The remainder of this chapter addresses that concern. I believe that my response to the pessimistic induction is one that scientific realists who disagree with me about the role of convergence and method may avail themselves of, and consequently, I frame my response to the pessimistic induction in terms of scientific realism generally, rather than in terms of my specific thesis that science progresses toward greater accuracy. In the final section of this chapter, I address the relationship between the present argument and the status of scientific realism.

Scientific anti-realism implies that no one knows that oxygen exists, and it follows that what scientists say about oxygen is not knowledge. Some anti-realists deny that what scientists say about oxygen is true; others claim that it might be true, but we have no reason to believe that it is. Others still claim that the existence of oxygen depends on a particular theoretical framework that partially constitutes reality; if so, the "existence" of oxygen depends on contingent facts about us, which, if they changed, would annihilate oxygen even though nothing independent of us changed in the process. Scientific realism implies that oxygen exists, that we know that it does, and that many of the things scientists say about oxygen are true. Let's call this tripartite realist claim *the realist view of oxygen*.

Since Larry Laudan first developed the pessimistic induction in 1980, it has been the site of considerable philosophical effort from both realists and anti-realists. Indeed, while philosophical attention to the underdetermination debate seems to have subsided, interest in the pessimistic induction has grown. A subset of realists (e.g. Ladyman and Ross), following John Worrall [Wor89], have embraced the pessimistic induction as a partial motivation for a variety of realism, structural realism. Kyle Stanford has rejuvenated the pessimistic induction in his recent book *Exceeding Our Grasp*.

A goal of this chapter is to investigate whether the pessimistic induction successfully blocks the realist view of oxygen, and to investigate the consequences of the result. If the pessimistic induction does not block the realist view of oxygen, then the pessimistic induction does not establish anti-realism because anti-realism implies that no one knows that oxygen exists, but the pessimistic induction does not establish that no one knows that oxygen exists. Furthermore, if realists can establish the realist view of oxygen, something less than full-blown realism but more than anti-realism is underway. This highlights the fact that scientific realism is not equivalent to the realist view of oxygen. One might be highly skeptical of science in general but accept the realist view of oxygen as an exception to the rule. Nevertheless, the realist view of oxygen is contested territory in the realism debate, and establishment or rejection of the realist view of oxygen would be a considerable victory for one side and a considerable defeat for the other.

§3.3 articulates the main commitments of realists and of anti-realists who accept the pessimistic induction; it also articulates my own commitments for the history that follows. §3.4 turns to historical science and the instrumental success of oxygen; I contrast that instrumental success with that of caloric, which has been a favorite topic of advocates of the pessimistic induction. §3.5 extracts the lessons of that history: the pessimistic induction fails to defeat the realist view of oxygen; however, it motivates important considerations in the realism debate, and illustrates that the issue between realists and anti-realists is a matter of where the margin lies. Instrumental success is a spectrum, at one end lies science that realists allege merits realist attitudes, while at the other end are instrumental failures; the question is how much instrumental success is enough for realism. Importantly, one argumentative path on behalf of the pessimistic induction turns on the debate about evidential underdetermination; finally, the methodology of the present discussion offers a new approach to philosophical discussion of science that may be profitable in the debate about realism and in other areas of philosophy of science.

3.3 Pessimism and Realism

The pessimistic induction attacks realists' basic argument for their view known as *the explanatory defense of realism*. The basic argument for realism says that the significant and widespread instrumental success of sciences provides convincing evidence that sciences correctly describe their domains, even where they describe their domains in terms of unobservable processes and entities; realists infer truth from instrumental success. Support for this inference derives from claiming that explanations of instrumental success that compete with a realistic explanation are decreasingly plausible as the instrumental success increases; according to the explanatory defense of realism, the plausibility of anti-realist explanations of instrumental success is inversely proportional to the degree of instrumental success itself. The explanatory defense links instrumental success and accuracy: realists claim that the best or only explanation of the instrumental successes of a science is that the science has accurately described its subject domain. This argument really has two different, related thrusts: first, its advocates think that anti-realist accounts of science strain credulity by asking us to suppose (for example) that there is no oxygen while nevertheless successfully describing multifarious phenomena in terms of oxygen, manipulating oxygen in experiments, and providing precise representations of oxygen itself; second, they see their account as possessing theoretical virtues that make realism a powerful explanatory theory.

The pessimistic induction attacks this realist inference from instrumental success by appealing to the history of instrumental successes in sciences we now regard as radically false. If the vast majority of past sciences enjoyed success similar to present sciences but were nevertheless radically false, the realist's inference from the successes of present sciences to their truth is undercut. Past radically false sciences enjoyed successes similar to present sciences. Hence, the realist inference is undercut.

The fundamental idea of the pessimistic induction is that the history of radically false but instrumentally successful science undercuts the realist inference to accuracy from instrumental success. What does this history need to look like in order for realists' explanatory defense to be undercut?

First, instrumentally successful radically false theories need to be numerous. If they aren't numerous, realists can cite them as proof of the fallibility of their explanatory defense. Because realists hold (indeed, insist) that their inference is fallible, it will be no surprise if some of its instances involve false conclusions even where the premises are true. It will be bad if these occur frequently, and it will be best if there is an explanation for the instrumental success absent accuracy. This will be especially pressing if later science deals with the same empirical regularities and observations as the earlier sciences. For those phenomena about which later science is silent, the lack of an explanation may seem more tolerable. However, in this chapter I am not concerned with the issue of the number of theories that form the basis of the pessimistic induction nor with the more general issue of the strength of the argument.[5] Second, the instrumental success of past radically false science needs to resemble the instrumental success of present instrumentally successful science. The pessimistic in-

---

[5]Some philosophers have recently charged that the pessimistic induction is fallacious. Peter Lewis [Lew01] points out that if the number of past false theories is much greater than the number of past true theories, the observed number of false successful theories may be larger than the observed number of past true theories. Mark Lange [Lan02] has noted that the pessimistic induction may be an instance of the turnover fallacy, which may be illustrated thus: suppose I know that half the ducks currently on the pond will not be on the pond tomorrow; it does not follow that each duck on the pond has a .5 probability of being on the pond tomorrow. See Saatsi [Saa05] for responses to Lewis and Lange.

duction hopes to project the failure (by realist lights) of past science onto present sciences; for the realist to find such projections legitimate (or, at least, pressing) past science must resemble present sciences that realists think are accurate. To be slightly more precise, past scientific instrumental successes must share with present science both degrees and types of instrumental success.

The pessimistic induction, thus presented, is not an objection to realism but to the argument for realism known as the explanatory defense of realism. But it is not hard to extend the argument to attack realism itself. At least with respect to unobservables, the only thing that could license realism is instrumental success. However, past sciences have enjoyed every variety of instrumental success while being radically false. Thus, no variety of instrumental success could warrant realism. The epistemic dimension to realism, that we have reasons to accept that some scientific representations of unobservables are accurate, cannot be maintained. (This treatment of the extension of the pessimistic induction is too cursory, but the present discussion is about the conclusion of the pessimistic induction, not extensions that depend upon it.)

Clarifications of scientific realism, instrumental success, and radical falsity are in order. *Scientific realism* says the established representations of mature sciences accurately represent nature, and we have good reasons to accept that those representations are accurate. Implicit in this definition is that the scope of accurate representation includes both observables and unobservables; this difference distinguishes realism from empiricism.[6] This definition concurs with standard ones, and my hope is to capture the shared commitment of scientific realists, who sometimes (perhaps frequently) dis-

---

[6]Empiricism itself is difficult to define because it has been advanced both as a thesis about meaning of scientific representations, as by logical positivists, and as a thesis about the acceptable commitments of science, as by constructive empiricists. Most contemporary empiricists seem to follow van Fraassen's constructive empiricism in taking the latter epistemic conception of empiricism. For realist criticisms of positivist empiricism, see Maxwell [Max62]. Van Fraassen [van80] offers the empiricist rejoinder that eschews their particularly linguistic variety of empiricism. Alan Musgrave [Mus85] is a good introduction to the realists' response to van Fraassen.

agree about details.⁷ I have not framed realism in terms of scientific theories, for there is room for realists to think that theories are not the principle sort of scientific representation. Realism is a view about the established components of mature sciences: realists need not be committed to accuracy at the frontiers of scientific research.

An *instrumental success* is just about any imaginable empirical success that a representation might have: explaining persistent regularities in nature or significant particular events; making correct predictions that are noteworthy in their precision, diversity, or novelty; unifying apparently heterogeneous phenomena; having a role in development of important technological advancements; being generally a part of successful scientific research projects.⁸ This may seem like a surprising and uncritical list—many of these standards are not even accepted by scientific anti-realists. However, according to the pessimistic induction, no matter how liberal one is with a standard of instrumental success, some past radically false theories have satisfied that standard. If this is not so, then realists defeat the pessimistic induction by pointing to successes that never belong to radically false theories. The realist would, of course, need to show that the type of instrumental success in question had at least some claim to truth-tracking, but realists' attempts to identify important forms of instrumental success, such as novel predictions [Psi99][Lep97], that belong to ultimately successful sciences but not to past radically false theories have typically seemed like epistemically credible successes. At least, no advocate of the pessimistic induction that I know of has admitted that novel predictions (for example) belong only to contem-

---

⁷Among realist views, Hacking's entity realism, which says that we have reason to believe that unobservable entities that scientists use in their experiments exist but not that models of those entities are accurate, is the most difficult to square with this definition. (See [Hac82] and [Hac83].) I have trouble seeing how Hacking can say that we don't know any descriptive claim about, for example, electrons except that they exist. Moreover, since Hacking disavows the explanatory defense, *his* entity realism is an aside for the present chapter. Resnik [Res94] discusses entity realism and its relation to descriptive claims and to the explanatory defense. With a look forward to §3.5, Hacking's view seems to be one that locates the margin of realism closer to skepticism.

⁸Comments on an early draft of this chapter recommended that I note that saying that oxygen is instrumentally successful may appear to be an alarming category mistake; those anticipating a clarification of this notion may jump to page 94.

porary science but argued that they cannot bear the epistemic weight that is placed upon them.

Being instrumentally successful is a matter of accumulating instrumental successes while avoiding or resolving failures; being instrumentally successful is, of course, a matter of degree. When trying to assess degrees of instrumental success, there are many procedures one could use. Indeed, confirmation just is a matter of how instrumental successes of various sorts relate to rational acceptance. Consequently, the measure we place on a set of instrumental successes is not in general a trivial matter. Nevertheless, we may repeat a point made earlier: the point of the pessimistic induction is that regardless of the form instrumental success of present science takes, past theories have enjoyed that level of instrumental success despite being radically false. Because the pessimistic induction alleges that no amount of instrumental success differentiates currently accepted theories from past theories we now regard as radically false, it obviates a burden to debate realists about what reasoning is appropriate to science. But it also means that the realist is not required to develop a careful account of confirmation to respond to the criticism. (This contrasts with the debate about underdetermination, where differences between realists and anti-realists have often been about the epistemic import of different varieties of instrumental success or the import of "super-empirical" virtues such as simplicity.) Realists have attempted to circumscribe instrumental successes that belong especially to ultimately successful sciences but not radically false ones [Psi99][Lep97], but that is not the strategy of the present chapter. I offer two much simpler measures of instrumental success: a count of individual instrumental successes discounted by unresolved individual failures, and a ratio of individual successes to unresolved individual failures.[9] This account of instrumental success is not a perfect one, but neither is it misleading; it forms a

---

[9]Note that we count types of success, not tokens. Repeatedly making the same correct prediction, for example, does not typically count as *greater* evidence; it merely shows an experimental success to be reproducible. Reproductions legitimate the initial result, but they don't increase the evidential significance of it.

good starting point for any discussion on the topic of confirmation. Most importantly, if it distorts the picture according to the pessimistic induction, advocates of the pessimistic induction need to say how it is unfair to their argument.

My way of understanding instrumental success raises the question, "How are we to understand the instrumental success of oxygen?" Oxygen, after all, is a stuff, and not the sort of thing we would call "instrumentally successful." The explanatory defense of realism appeals to the success of sciences as evidence of the accuracy of their representations, but oxygen isn't even the right sort of thing to be instrumentally successful. This is, strictly speaking, correct, but *representations* of oxygen are the sort of thing that can be instrumentally successful. A representation of oxygen has an instrumental success if it has a role in instrumentally successful scientific research.[10] Oxygen is instrumentally successful to the degree that the count of instrumental successes of representations of oxygen greatly exceeds the count of unresolved instrumental failures of representations of oxygen; less precisely but more succinctly: oxygen is instrumentally successful to the degree that the count of its successes is greater than the count of its failures. Note that according to this definition, representations of oxygen may be successful even when the research that produces success is not on a theory *of oxygen*. Oxygen has an instrumental failure if a representation of oxygen coupled with plausible additional assumptions conflicts with well-established scientific thought, or implies observations that are not detected through means of detecting them. Note that failures are not here treated as reasons to reject a representation or entities it is committed to, but only as counting against their instrumental success.

Radical falsity involves significant descriptive inaccuracy, usually in key concepts that purport to refer to entities or mechanisms which turn out not to exist. Laudan

---

[10] A representation is one of oxygen if the speaker intends to refer to oxygen. The referential intentions of scientists are a subtle matter beyond the scope of this chapter; Kitcher [Kit93, sections 3.7 and 4.4] offers an extensive treatment of the subject.

The term 'oxygen' is ambiguous because it names both a molecular compound as well as a chemical element. Herein, I use the term 'oxygen' or 'O_2' for the molecular form and 'atomic oxygen' or 'O' for the atomic form.

[Lau81, 33] offers a famous list of radically false theories from the history of science, and at least some of those include established representations from mature sciences, such as the electromagnetic ether and caloric theory of heat.[11] If a theory is radically false, then it is not even approximately true.[12]

The pessimistic induction is successful only if science has a history of instrumental success despite radical falsity *and that success is similar to success of present established science.* To the degree that radically false but instrumentally successful sciences are similar in their instrumental success to those sciences that realists accept, the pessimistic induction undercuts the explanatory defense of realism. So, what is the history of science like?

3.4 Brief Histories: Oxygen and Caloric

In order to assess the history, I contrast oxygen with caloric. That choice is not arbitrary: various accounts of heat that involve caloric are typically held to be among the best example of past instrumentally successful scientific research committed to something radically false.[13] I now turn to the instrumental success of oxygen and compare that with the instrumental success of caloric. The result, I shall claim, is that the instrumental success of oxygen far outstrips that of caloric.

In the late 18th and 19th centuries, caloric was an important part of scientific

---

[11] Laudan's list also includes the crystalline spheres of ancient astronomy and humoral theory of medicine. Many realists rightly responded that these theories were not really similar to present science in their instrumental successes.

[12] This too has been challenged. Imagine that some theoretical entity of a theory turns out to be multiply realized and does not seem like a natural kind in light of the manner of its realizations. It would thus be tempting to say that the entity in question did not exist, but that descriptions in terms of it were approximately true. Hardin and Rosenberg [HR82] raise this concern and argue that genes are exactly this sort of thing.

[13] It so happens that one early exposition of caloric is also the early exposition of oxygen, viz., Antoine Lavoisiers's *Elements of Chemistry*. This fact is merely coincidental, and my argument does not turn on the fact that, of two key entities in Lavoisier's system, oxygen has survived while caloric has perished. (However, this fact seems problematic for social constructivist accounts of scientific development, since it is quite hard to see why merely social forces should happily admit oxygen while ultimately rejecting caloric when the two share an origin.)

thinking about heat.[14] The fundamental idea of these accounts is that heat is, or is caused by, a material fluid, caloric, that is released in phenomena of heat. The alternatives to caloric theories were mechanical theories which claimed that phenomena of heat were, or were caused by, motions of particles.[15] There was no unitary *theory of caloric*; as with any (putative) entity that scientists discuss, theoretical claims about it are advanced, retracted, and debated among those whose research it involves.

Lavoisier's 1789 *Elements of Chemistry* is a critical work in the history of science and is most famous today for articulating the first chemical theory in which oxygen plays a prominent role. It is thus an important instrumental success of caloric, for Lavoisier's chemical theory could not be made to work without it. Indeed, caloric was more important than oxygen to chemical theory [Lil48, 632]. Combustion was a major subject of Lavoisier's chemistry, and he sought to account for two aspects of the phenomena: (as is well known) the absorption of part of the air in the process, and (as is less well known) the emission of light and heat.[16] According to Lavoisier, oxygen *gas* was a combination of a solid, oxygen, and caloric. The process of combustion separated oxygen from caloric, causing the emission of heat, and combining oxygen into the combusted substance, thereby accounting for the increase of weight after calcination.

---

[14]I acknowledge a debt to Hasok Chang, whose careful scholarship in [Cha03] and [Cha04] directed me to excellent references, S. Lilley [Lil48] and Robert Fox [Fox71]. Chang's work itself is also a good source for history.

[15]While these theories were alternatives, many scientists seemed to regard both as incomplete [Men61][Lil48], and it is not clear that the two were always considered *rivals*, in the sense of being incompatible [Men61]. Lilley [Lil48, 631] claims that "faith in [the material theory of heat] was much less than, for example, our faith today in the quantum theory." Note that Lilley writes this in 1948, only 35 years after Bohr publishes his theory of the hydrogen atom and 23 years after Schrödinger and Heisenberg present their quantum theories.

[16]Within the phlogiston theory that Lavoisier's system eventually replaced, phlogiston played both of these roles; the systematic confusion of heat with combustion was an element of nearly all accounts of either phenomenon until Lavoisier, and was an element of every phlogiston theory from Stahl onward. In the context of this dissertation, this is an important respect in which Lavoissier's system seems to be *more accurate* than Stahl's or Priestly's. Herein lies, I believe, a respect in which an apparent ontological commitment to something that does not exist might nevertheless improve the accuracy of a science over its rivals.

Because of this precise account of caloric in combustion, Lavoisier was able to propose techniques for measuring caloric. He attempted to determine the quantity of caloric that combined with oxygen to form a gas, the quantity released in combustion of each substance, and, by subtraction the quantity that remained in the product. Caloric provided a good quantitative theory of specific and latent heats.[17] In many respects, latent heat resembles chemical combination, for heat seems to be absorbed or emitted during state changes in matter. Lilley [Lil48] concludes that given the limits of empirical knowledge around 1800, caloric offered quite comprehensive treatments the main explanatory targets of the day's scientists; the generation of heat by work and the converse were *not* among those targets, though scientists were aware of the issue and many sought to resolve it.

Further accounts of chemical and physical phenomena in terms of caloric offered additional promising results. Especially noteworthy is the adiabatic expansion of gases. Caloric theories offered an account of this phenomenon. Perhaps surprisingly, caloric theories were thus able to offer a correction to Newton's derivation of the speed of sound that eliminated some of the error between Newton's value and experimental observations. Moreover, caloric was not idle in the account; Chang [Cha03] notes that mathematically precise description of properties of caloric were essential to the derivation.[18] In particular, caloric was thought to be self-repelling and precise mathematical descriptions of this self-repellent nature were required for the derivations.[19]

A discussion of Laplace's work on the speed of sound will illustrate the precision

---

[17]Latent heat is the heat that is exchanged in state transitions of matter. For ice to melt, for example, a certain amount of heat must be added to it which does not change the temperature of the ice. Except near the points where it changes state, adding heat to water (whether solid, liquid or gas) raises or lowers its temperature in a linear way. Specific heat is heat required to raise the temperature of a body.

[18]Psillos [Psi99] claims that the existence of caloric was an idle assumption that played no positive role in the derivation; Chang [Cha03] convincingly responds to that claim, and shows that it is mistaken.

[19]Self-repellent natures sound metaphysically abstruse; the reader is reminded that self-attracting natures were associated with massive bodies at that time, and similar forces of attraction and repulsion were known in magnetic and electrical phenomena.

and detail of calorists' work.[20] Laplace believed that a gas consisted of massive particles; whereas he accepted Newtonian accounts of masses, this required an explanation of why the particles don't coalesce, but instead form an elastic collection. In 1799, he wrote a paper in which he suggested that the particles of a gas repel each other with a force proportional to $1/r$, where r is the distance between them. In 1821, he attempted to show that the quantity of caloric contained in a particle of a gas accounted for this repulsive force. To do this, Laplace attempted to show that the pressure, P, of a gas must be proportional to $\rho^2 c^2$, where ρ is the density of the gas and c the quantity of caloric in each of its particles. Laplace additionally explained constancy of temperature by supposing that it results from a dynamic equilibrium of radiation and absorption of caloric from the particles. The density of radiant caloric he supposed to be equal to a function $\Pi(t)$, and a fraction of this caloric, q, (dependent on the gas in question) would be absorbed while the remainder would be proportional to c and to ρc, from which it followed that

$$\rho c^2 = q\Pi(t). \tag{3.1}$$

This equation (3.1) may appear entirely gratuitous, but several important phenomenological gas laws follow from it: Boyle's law, Guy-Lussac's law, and Dalton's law of partial pressures.[21]

Caloric encountered some failures as well.[22] One that was known from the late

---

[20]Laplace's work appears in an 1821 paper 'Sur l'attraction des sphères, et la répulsion des fluides élastiques' and, in a revised from, volume five of *Traité méchanique céleste*, but I have found no English translations of these works. The present exposition relies on [Fox71, 165–77]. Hasok Chang has confirmed in written communication that Laplace's later works on heat, as well as his contemporaries', remain untranslated.

[21]The derivation seems possibly to be *ad hoc*, for it is likely that the assumptions that allowed Laplace to produce eqn. 3.1 were tailored for the derivation. It strikes me that it is nevertheless a merit that it produces the derivations, and I have promised herein not to distinguish among the varieties of instrumental success. There were some independent confirmations of the assumptions, but, though they were taken to be empirically supported at the time, the assumptions needed for that independent confirmation were later shown false. See Fox [Fox71, 173].

[22]These failures were important scientific problems in their day, and had varying influence on the scientific community. I do not here judge whether these failures should have had a different effect than the ones that they had. They are failures, but I make no claim that they are *decisive* failures.

18th century was that indefinite amounts of heat seem to be produced by work, such as by friction. If caloric is a material substance, it should be exhaustible, and that means that friction should not produce indefinite amounts of heat. The problem was acknowledged by calorists, and they sought solutions, but no solution was universally accepted (even momentarily) among them. Particular caloric theories encounter problems particular to them; Laplace's was the height of precise work by calorists, but the correction it implied for Newton's speed of sound obviously disagreed with experiment.[23]

It is difficult to know where to begin with oxygen. Unlike caloric, whose role was mostly restricted to chemistry and closely related physics, oxygen is represented in sciences from physiology to physics. Perhaps a survey of the most pedestrian phenomena involving oxygen is in order: oxygen is part of the Earth's atmosphere and is taken up by burning substances in common phenomena of combustion; it is also necessary for respiration in living organisms, and its role in respiration distinguishes it from other gases, such as nitric oxide, which support combustion; 21% of Earth's atmosphere is oxygen; 89% of the mass of water is oxygen, which is chemically one part atomic oxygen and two parts hydrogen; atomic oxygen is the most common element in the earth's crust, which is about 46% atomic oxygen; oxygen is the third most common element in our solar system; aerobic respiration, the principle form of cellular metabolism, typically proceeds by chemical reaction of oxygen with glucose; atomic oxygen has three stable isotopes, of which ^{16}O is by far the most common; it is synthesized through fusion of helium and carbon, $^{12}_{6}C + ^{4}_{2}He \rightarrow ^{16}_{8}O$.

More contemporary successes of oxygen are seen by surveying the literature in scientific journals. The proceedings of a 1974 symposium on measuring oxygen [DBB76] contained 19 articles on measuring oxygen; here are some of the titles:

> Gas chromatographic measurements of oxygen in aqueous solutions

---
[23]See [Fox71, 168].

> Oxygen measurement by the Cartesian diver technique
>
> The measurement of dissolved oxygen in continuous fermentations
>
> Quantitative micro-respirometry of biological tissue *in vitro* by use of hemoglobin spectrophotometry
>
> Some properties and applications of zirconia-based solid-electrolyte cells
>
> Mass spectrometric determination of oxygen kinetics in biochemical systems

As these titles indicate, measurement and manipulation of oxygen can be found in numerous scientific fields, and measurements involve various properties of oxygen in myriad environments (biological tissue, aqueous solutions, and fermenting beer). The title on zirconia-based cells does not even suggest that it is about oxygen, but the first sentence of the article reads "Solid oxygen-ion conductors like stabilized zirconia can be used in oxygen-generating (or pumping) cells as well as in voltage-generating measuring cells."[24]

3.5 Lessons from History

Has oxygen been instrumentally successfully? Monumentally. The catalog of representations of oxygen above includes a paltry selection of oxygen's successes. Indeed, providing a count of the successes of oxygen would be a herculean task. Here, to illustrate the magnitude of oxygen's success, I have tried to illustrate the diverse fields in which representations, measurements, and manipulations of oxygen have a role. That diversity itself has been alleged to be a form of instrumental success, but the present argument is not intended to rest on that claim. The point of appealing to the

---

[24]Shaughan Lavine has noted that these points about the instrumental success of oxygen are largely anachronistic, since these successes accumulate largely after caloric has been replaced with a mechanical theory of heat. This is correct, but the present point is that oxygen possesses these instrumental successes, not that all of them have been a part of any one scientist's acceptance of oxygen, nor that they were the instrumental successes that convinced 19th century scientists to accept oxygen.

scope of successes of oxygen is to give a sense of the number of successes that oxygen enjoys.

Was caloric instrumentally successful? Certainly it was. I have cataloged several successes here. Hasok Chang (whose research has helped to inform the present discussion) concurs, and offers the following list of important successes of caloric: "the flow of heat toward equilibrium, the expansion of matter by heating, latent heat in changes of state, the elasticity of gases and the fluidity of liquids, the heat released and absorbed in chemical reactions, combustion, the radiation of heat, and the gas laws" [Cha03, 907].

Was the instrumental success of caloric close to that of oxygen? No—not even remotely. Whatever the pessimistic induction amounts to, it cannot claim that representations of caloric were as instrumentally successful as representations of oxygen. Because the instrumental success of oxygen far outstrips that of caloric, the explanatory defense of the realist view of oxygen is not undercut by the pessimistic induction on the history of caloric. Perhaps the history of science offers a better case against the realist view of oxygen, but if so, advocates of the pessimistic induction have been curiously silent about them. Caloric is routinely offered as an exemplary case. Among scientific commitments alleged to be radically false, only the electromagnetic ether has been said to be similarly successful.

Many early instrumental successes of oxygen involved theories that were badly inaccurate about some of its features. Lavoisier imagined that oxygen was vital to phenomena of acidity and supposed that it was a unitary substance. Oxygen is not vital to acidity, and it is not unitary—it is made up of two parts of atomic oxygen. This suggests an objection: an explanatory defense of oxygen is not forthcoming, since its successes often depended upon false descriptions of oxygen. However, such an objection is difficult to make out, for both of these examples may seem to the realist to be approximately true. With respect to the unitary nature of oxygen, most of the known chemical phenomena with pure oxygen adequately represent it as unitary, for O_2 behaves very much as though it were indivisible. Moreover, this issue was resolved (by Avogadro) in 1811. The issue with respect to acidity is similar; Lavoisier indeed struggled with "muriatic acid" from which he could not extract oxygen, but his hypothesis that oxygen is the principle of acidity led to the discovery of over twenty-five acids between 1775 and 1790; the number of known acids before that time was five or six [Mus76, 198].[25]

It might be objected that, while the instrumental success of caloric did not actually rival that of oxygen, it would have were thermodynamics not to have replaced it: The history of science is written by victors, and retrospective appearance of special success is unavoidable because once there is a victor, all research occurs within its framework. With no rival, all the successes belong to the victor and there are no detractors to draw attention to its failures. According to this objection, the appearance of special success is a necessary but epistemically irrelevant by-product of scientific development.

If this objection is a necessary component of the pessimistic induction, it is a considerably more complex argument than it was originally. It is also considerably more dubious. We have entered a realm of speculative history about what science would have been like if caloric had not been replaced with thermodynamics.[26] The speculation is that if thermodynamics had not replaced it, the instrumental success of caloric would be similar to that of oxygen, but it is unclear what the antecedent of this claim describes. Some factor must differentiate that world from this one, but it is not clear what that factor is. It is not a change in the unobservable world described by our theory, for that would be a change relevant to the truth of caloric and thermodynamics, and the point of the pessimistic induction is that truth is not relevant to success. If it is a change about the observable world, i.e., in what

---

[25] The term 'oxygen' means acid maker. Muriatic acid is now recognized as hydrochloric acid and contains no atomic oxygen.

[26] Very confident realists might even respond "Caloric would have done very well in such a world, for the closest world in which caloric succeeds is one in which 'caloric' refers to the caloric that exists there."

observations we would make in thus and such scientific context that differs from those we would make in this world, the realist will say that the question has been begged: does a difference to the unobservable world make the difference? Merely to assume that there can be changes to the observable world without changes to the unobservable one is illegitimate.

A more pressing issue regarding this counter-factual conditional is that evidence for it is not forthcoming. Are we to believe that any theoretical framework at all can be fitted to any observational data at all? And not merely fitted but in a satisfying way?[27] A positive answer in each case is an implication of supposing that caloric would have been as successful as oxygen if it had received due research attention. It is sometimes remarked about the problem of underdetermination of theories that the problem gets the scientific problem wrong: it is not narrowing the field of *copious* theoretical alternatives that is hard, but finding *one* theory that fits all the relevant data. Regardless of its merit in the underdetermination debate, that observation seems correct and this infirms the thought that any theoretical framework can be made to work. Scientific work is hard, and the claim that any data can be satisfactorily fitted to any framework ignores this fact. It is worth emphasizing here that caloric theories offered no (even briefly) agreed upon account of the production of heat through work for sixty years during which scientists developed caloric models of heat.

There is a rejoinder available to the anti-realist, and it points to a significant issue. The rejoinder is: any theoretical framework at all can be fitted to any observational data at all, though not in a satisfactory way; however, whether a framework is satisfactory or not is a matter of *pragmatic* standards that have no epistemic significance whatsoever. Simplicity and scope are the sorts of features that make it impossible to accommodate any data at all in a satisfactory way,[28] but (according to this objection)

---

[27]This is an issue of holism in the philosophy of science and whether observations are logically related to particular statements or (in Duhem's terms) "theoretical groups." It is worth noting that Laudan [Lau84] explicitly rejects holist theses.

[28]This is, of course, a substantive claim that empirical data can be fitted if we ignore the pragmatic

simplicity and scope are pragmatic, not epistemic, considerations. Many realists will not be happy with this claim, for they have discussed and rejected it: this is the debate about underdetermination of theory by evidence. If the pessimistic induction is defended by appeal to the epistemic insignificance of considerations that make theories unable to cope with the relevant data, the success of the pessimistic induction depends on the success of underdetermination arguments.[29]

The pessimistic induction does not defeat the realist view of oxygen, so it fails to establish anti-realism. However, the pessimistic induction does seem to move us in an anti-realist direction. As we have seen, instrumental successes accrued to caloric despite the fact that caloric does not exist. Properties ascribed to caloric and described in precise mathematical detail were important to the instrumental success of caloric. Caloric was not an idle metaphysical postulate of scientific research—it did important scientific work.

The pessimistic induction reveals that the threshold of instrumental success for realism is harder to cross than realists previously recognized. For opaque reasons, discussions of scientific realism and the pessimistic induction have tended to carve the question in such a way that realism is all-or-nothing. It was not the intent of thus carving that we should ignore that our evidence is a matter of degree; nevertheless, that seems often to have been the effect. How else could discussion of pessimistic inductions have ignored the gap between instrumental success of oxygen and instrumental success of caloric?

The question of scientific realism regards the margin: where is the boundary between enough and too little instrumental success? Even thus formulated, something

---

considerations in question; realists might debate it, but I won't debate it here.

[29]Stanford [Sta06] has recently argued that the situation of the pessimistic induction is one of persistent transient underdetermination; that view holds that at any given point in the development of science, there will be unconsidered alternatives to the received view that are evidentially just as well-supported by the available evidence as the received view. It is not part of Stanford's view that any theory can satisfactorily be accommodated to any evidence, so his view does not rely on the counter-factual conditional that caloric would have been as successful as thermodynamics if it were given sufficient research effort.

is missing, for just as instrumental success is a matter of degree, so is confidence; the margin itself is consequently vague; perhaps the penumbral region between them is vast. Historical reflection on scientific success should inform our understanding of the relationship between success and accuracy. Prior to historical reflection, those with realist dispositions are overly optimistic about the connection. Considerations from the pessimistic induction move the boundary closer to more skeptical positions. The space of scientific work that we should regard in a realist way thus shrinks, though as we have seen, it does not disappear.

I have not walked the avenue of underdetermination yet in this dissertation, and here I wish only to suggest where that avenue leads. One variety of underdetermination argument simply advances global skepticism by arguing that our evidence underdetermines nearly everything we believe. Within the realism debate, this variety of underdetermination is uninteresting, for it is a threat to accounts of science that allege it produces any knowledge whatsoever; however philosophically formidable global skepticism is, it does not distinguish among rivals in the realism debate. Interesting varieties of underdetermination argument claim that certain varieties of scientific representation suffer a special problem of underdetermination, such as, for example, that representations of observables underdetermine representations of unobservables [van80]. The success of such arguments requires that that they can be coherently advanced without collapsing into global skepticism: observations underdetermine observables, too, and the empiricists' view collapses into global skepticism unless they say what epistemic considerations distinguish observation-observables underdetermination from observables-unobservables underdetermination. In particular, it should be asked whether the realist view of oxygen is underdetermined in a way that the relationship between observations and observables is not underdetermined.

Because Kyle Stanford [Sta06] has recently formulated the pessimistic induction in terms of underdetermination, I should mention him here. On his view, scientists persistently fail to consider alternative scientific accounts, and the available evidence supports these unconsidered rival accounts just as well as those with which scientists actually work. If two accounts are equally well-supported, the evidence (in Stanford's terms) transiently underdetermines the choice between them. Hence, Stanford claims, on the basis of this history of transient underdetermination, that we can conclude that the present is transiently underdetermined as well. Stanford's argument deserves more careful attention than present space allows. In the present context it suffices to note that it suffers from the short-coming of the pessimistic induction as it is standardly formulated: on the basis of past scientific accounts that are significantly less instrumentally successful than many present ones, we are supposed to conclude something about considerably more successful science. Where Stanford's argument fails is that no radically false theory that we know of enjoyed oxygen's instrumental success, so it fails to undercut the realist view of oxygen.

The present discussion raises the question "whither realism?" What components of science does instrumental success support, and which particular components of actual science admit or require a realist attitude?—where is the margin? It is for another work to answer these questions fully, for they either require considerations new to this essay or a long explanation of how the present considerations are sufficient to answer the question (which, I suspect, they are not.) A comment or two is nevertheless in order. With regard to the former, more general question, I suspect that no general claim about what sorts of components of science instrumental successes support will be forthcoming. If and whether it is primarily entities, processes, structures, laws, mechanisms, models, implications of laws, or implications of models, that deserve realist treatment, seems to be a contingent matter, and I see no call for *ex ante* prejudice. It depends on what things we use successfully, and that is not something we know in advance. Regarding the latter question, which particular components of actual science require or admit a realist attitude is partly an empirical question about the instrumental successes they enjoy. It strains credulity to suppose that we know that oxygen exists but that we know nothing descriptive about it, so present considerations show that some cluster of our beliefs about oxygen are also true. But it is a matter of important details, not settled by the present discussion, which beliefs those are. Moreover, we should avoid epistemological hubris, and be ready to confess when our descriptive claims are somewhat speculative.

These comments may suggest that realism has become unfortunately piecemeal.[30] The promise of realism was to give us science that produced knowledge of the unobservable world, and understanding of the world in general. Realism, it was alleged, also provided an explanation of scientific success that now may appear to be eliminated. We are left with a view that science sometimes, somewhere finds the truth, but little guide to when or where, or whether it might happen again. Perhaps the reasons to champion the cause of realism are gone. One might wonder what's left to fuss about. One thing to fuss about is the truth. If the weaker realism these considerations suggest is a less exciting theory than the one some hoped for, it is still the truth. Moreover, though realist optimism about present science may diminish in light of these considerations, optimism about the future might remain. Realism avoids becoming piecemeal if realists can establish that science will increase its store of instrumental success regarding those accurate representations it presently possesses. A significant topic for realists becomes how science makes progress. This has, of course, been the central aim of this dissertation.

---

[30] Arthur Fine [Fin91] makes this complaint. Ernan McMullan [McM91] offers a response.

CHAPTER 4

THE AIMS OF SCIENCE OR LACK THEREOF

Philosophical literature on scientific progress frequently frames progress in terms of aims of science: science, we are told, progresses when it achieves or promotes its aim. Coupling this with a theory of the aim of science delivers a substantive theory of scientific progress. Within the framework of aims of science, a theory of scientific progress must thus specify two things. First, it must specify the aim or aims of science. Second, it must specify the relationship between aims and progress. It will not do, for example, to say just that science aims at truth, for there are many ways science can develop regarding truth. Theories that specify the vague aim *truth* need to state what relationship to truth pairs of stages of science must have in order to be progressive. Less vague aims for a monistic theory, such as the aim *to accumulate truth*, will deliver a straightforward relation between pairs of stages of science. (On this, more below.)

The framework of the aims of science has either implicitly or explicitly been the framework of most philosophy of scientific progress. Ilkka Niiniluoto is perfectly explicit:

> 'Progress' is a normative or goal-relative—rather than purely descriptive—term: saying that the step from one theory A to another theory B constitutes progress means that B is an improvement of A in some respect. In this sense, 'progress' can be contrasted with such neutral terms as 'development', and *a philosophical analysis of scientific progress is tantamount to a specification of the aims of science.* [Nii84, 75–76, emphasis mine]

Niiniluoto expresses the orthodoxy about scientific progress. Two points (to be challenged in this chapter) are worth noting: first, orthodoxy assumes that science has aims; second, orthodoxy assumes that improvement of science and achieving aims of science are identical. Phillip Kitcher's *The Advancement of Science* is another example: "Our primary prescriptive tasks are to give an account of the goals of science and to derive from it a theory of what constitutes progress in science, to understand how individuals ought to behave and how their social relations should be designed to facilitate attainment of those goals." [Kit93, 61] Philosophers that haven't explicitly endorsed the framework of aims seem to assume that certain features would be progressive. Jarret Leplin [Lep84], for example, occasionally mentions "goals" of science, but mostly assumes some value in truth.

Even where philosophers of science are unconcerned with progress, aims of science are prominent. In the most prominent anti-realist work in recent philosophy of science, Bas van Fraassen [van80] offers no account of scientific progress. However, his formulations of scientific realism—probably the most widely known in philosophical literature—and constructive empiricism—his preferred alternative to realism—both make reference to aims:

> Science aims to give us, in its theories, a literally true story of what the world is like; and acceptance of a scientific theory involves the belief that it is true. [van80, 8]

> Science aims to give us theories that are empirically adequate; and acceptance of a theory involves, as belief, only that it is empirically adequate. [van80, 12]

The debate surrounding the rationality of science has taken for granted that scientific rationality involves scientific aims: champions of scientific rationality argue that science is well-designed for achieving its aims; their opponents argue that scientific development is the result of social processes unconnected to those aims.[1]

---

[1]The debate about scientific rationality is considerably more complex than this short discussion reveals. Realists and empiricists have tended toward the rationalist camp; the sociology of science

Besides framing a theory of progress, aims of science are connected with a separate issue of evaluating science—setting aside the issue of making progress, the difference between good and bad scientific work is sometimes stated in terms of satisfying or promoting a scientific aim. It is in this vein that van Fraassen offers a brief discussion of the aims of science in *The Scientific Image*. There in discussing 'aims' as part of his formulation of realism he writes:

> The correct statement [of scientific realism] says... that it is the aim of science to [tell a true story]. The aim of science is of course not to be identified with the individual scientists' motives. The aim of the game of chess is to checkmate your opponent; but the motive for playing may be fame, gold and glory. What the aim is determines what counts as success in the enterprise as such... [van80, 8]

For van Fraassen, the aim of an activity (in sense in which the activity of science has an aim) is what determines the success conditions of the activity. No doubt success conditions or other sorts of evaluative criteria are what many philosophers have had in mind in the discussion of aims in the realism debate.

Despite its prominence in philosophy of science, the claim that science aims is not clear: science is not an agent; it has no cognitive states; consequently, it does not have aims in the same sense that people have aims. The aims of science deserve philosophical attention. The foregoing conversation reveals two important senses in which science might be alleged to have aims. Quite generally speaking, aims of science are alleged to be the ultimate goals of scientific activity, so that, by reference to these goals, scientists direct their scientific research, or, at least, by reference to these goals

---

has been the source of anti-rationalists. Both camps seem to agree that science aims (or purports to aim) at something epistemic, but disagree about the process of scientific development. However, rationalists differ about the relationship between aims and rationality. Early rationalist accounts had aims direct scientific activity, but subsequent rationalist accounts (e.g., Kitcher [Kit93]) have moved away from this view. The rationality of science is a topic of chapter 5 of this dissertation.

we understand the proper structure of scientific institutions and methods.² This gives rise to two implications of the claim that science aims: first, as a matter of descriptive fact, scientific activity (either at the individual or social level) is organized around its aims; second, as a matter of evaluation, good science contributes, ultimately, to the achievement of scientific aims. Both of these implications are false, as we shall see.

In this chapter, I give the aims of science their deserved attention. By the end of the chapter, it will be clear that science has no aims: there are no over-arching goals that organize scientific activity, nor are there evaluative criteria that apply to all scientific research. However, even if science aimed, aims wouldn't produce a theory of scientific progress. Aims are supposed to connect to progress by grounding evaluative claims about science. That connection is hazy, and significant philosophical work would remain (if science were to aim) to connect aims to progress.

4.1 Does Science Have Aims?

In this section, I consider three proposals regarding what facts determine the aims of science. Because no writers have systematically treated the determination of the aims of science, I must try to do them justice as I put words in their mouths.³ Some philosophers who've employed the phrase "aims of science" in their work will be able to agree with everything I say below. Others may have some re-thinking to do. However, the goal of rejecting aims of science is not to attack a cherished thesis of philosophers: the thesis is not cherished, it is *de facto* orthodoxy.

The accounts of the aims of science I consider are: aims of science are shared aims of scientists; aims of science are explanations of scientific norms; aims of science

---

²This is the view of Kitcher, [Kit93].

³Don Falis [Fal07] has written on the subject of group cognitive goals generally, but does not specifically address the issue of the group cognitive goals of science. His concern in [Fal07] is with technical problems about the assignment of goals or aims to groups, not with the empirical problem of whether scientific communities satisfy the conditions laid out in various proposals about group cognitive goals.

are brute facts. Against the former two, I argue aims are underdetermined by the supposed facts that produce them. The final view is dialectically unacceptable and engenders skepticism.

4.1.1 Reductionism

Suppose the aims of science are the shared aims of scientists; this account reduces aims of science to aims of scientists. It is a natural way to spell-out the aims of science without making them curious entities. It employs a general strategy for applying 'aims' to non-agents: the aims of the non-agent are those of the agents suitably involved with the non-agents. For example, one way to understand a claim like 'The Declaration of Independence aims to liberate the colonies from English rule' is to understand that as a claim about the aims of signatories. Of course, not every aim of a signatory will be an aim of the Declaration. Some signatories may have aimed at forming a decentralized republic while others aimed at a federal system; it is aims about which there is agreement which would be aims of the Declaration. Moreover, it is those aims that they have *with* the Declaration that are aims *of* the Declaration: even if all of the signatories aim at eudaimonea, unless they aim at eudaimonea in drafting and signing the Declaration (a dubious proposition), eudaimonea is not an aim of the Declaration.[4] The reductive view says that aims of science are to aims of scientists as aims of the Declaration of Independence are to aims of its signatories.

In order to have a clear basis for the discussion of aims of scientists, it is helpful to think about aims in general, and relate them to a similar psychological state, goals.[5] In trying to complete a task, a person must often do many things; some of those things are in service to other things, done because they conduce to achieving something else, while other things are done for their own sake. A thing that someone tries to do

---

[4] 'Happiness' in 'The pursuit of happiness' is probably best understood as eudaimonea.

[5] Much of what follows is a somewhat stipulative account of the way in which I wish to use the term 'aims' and 'goals'. I don't know of any place that the particular usage here has been canonized, but it seems a natural way of making our language precise.

is a goal. A *primary goal* is a goal that is not adopted in service of accomplishing another goal. A *subgoal* is a goal adopted in service of another goal. A subgoal may be adopted in service of a primary goal or another subgoal. For example, a writer decides to revise his story. He adopts the goal of rewriting it, i.e. rewriting it is a primary goal for him. To do this, he decides to read the story and make notes about to how to re-express what needs re-expressing. Figuring out what needs re-expressing is a subgoal for him. After reading the story, he decides that the story has organizational problems and decides to reorganize it. He now has two subgoals, re-expressing and reorganizing. To re-express, he decides he needs to start from scratch on the most troubled part. He now has a subgoal in service to the subgoal of re-expressing.

The aims of a scientist are her primary goals. Because scientists engage in complex tasks, they will almost always posses subgoals of truth or knowledge. But this does not substantiate that truth or knowledge is an aim of the scientist any more than a scientist's persistent subgoals of doing mathematical computations substantiates that the scientist aims at applying mathematics.[6] Consider a similar case: because bankers engage in complex tasks, they will almost always have subgoals of truth or knowledge. But this does not substantiate the (obviously false) claim that banking aims at truth or knowledge. Subgoals, even if persistently occurring, are not the same as aims.

We are now ready to state a principle that connects the aims of scientists to the aims of science at a time:

> Science aims at x at time t if and only if, at t, x is a primary goal of a significant majority of scientists.

Some might demand a stronger principle requiring that, at t, x is a primary goal of all scientists (rather than a significant majority). I see no reason to set the bar so high.

---

[6]Some scientists do aim at applying mathematics. However, those that do have the application of mathematics as a primary goal, not merely a subgoal; the primary goal/subgoal distinction helps us clarify which scientists aim to apply mathematics and which simply apply it.

Moreover, I see reason not to. Science is a human endeavor and sometimes messy; rather than requiring some level of total homogeneity, it is better to admit that some exceptions will arise. If one historical scientist cared about different things than his compatriots, it should not level the reductionist view.

Some will be concerned with the vagueness of 'significant majority' and wonder what standard this is. I don't think that the vagueness here is problematic; on behalf of the reductivist about scientific aims, I argue that what majority is needed depends in part on circumstances. If 67% of scientists aim at x, while 32% reject that aim, the reductivist should deny that science aims at x. But if 67% aim at x while the rest are indifferent about x, it's plausible that science aims at x.[7]

I think that the reductive principle above is the best option for reducing aims of science at particular times to aims of scientists at particular times. What remains for the reductivist, of course, is to characterize the standing aims of science through the past and into the future. To do this, the natural approach is to ask what it is for science to aim during an interval of time. On the reductivist view, it seems, roughly, that science aims at something during an interval just if scientists aim (for the most part) at that thing at each time in the interval. More precisely: science aims at x during an interval of time $[t, t']$ if and only if for the preponderance of times in $[t, t']$, science aims at x.

The requirement of a preponderance of times should be strictly upheld. If, for example, there are long intervals during which scientists don't aim at x and long intervals where they do, the spirit of the reductive view should identify changing aims of science, rather than attempting some means of showing that science aimed at x all along. Brief departures from aiming at x can be tolerated, and certain conditions (perhaps, for example, scientific controversies) might allow the reductivist to explain

---

[7]Ultimately, I offer the present account because I think that it is the best one that the reductivist can offer. If the present discussion is too generous and the vagueness of 'significant majority' is problematic, so much the worse for the reductivist account of the aims of science.

away the apparent brief abandonment of a set of aims. Nevertheless, a genuinely reductivist view is hostage to actual aims of actual scientists.

On the reductive view of aims of science, the interval $[t, t']$ encompasses the whole of science. Above, we specified what it was for science to aim at a time. The final result for the reductivist view is:

The Reductivist Principle

Science aims at x during an interval of time $[t, t']$ if and only if for the preponderance of times in $[t, t']$, science aims at x.

Reductivism about aims of science allows both pluralism and monism about the aims. If exactly one x satisfies the reductivist principle, science has one aim. If more than one does, science has more than one aim. On the reductivist proposal, the aims of science are hostage to scientists's actual aims: multiple aims mean a pluralist theory, a single aim means a monist theory. If scientists exhibit preferences regarding their aims, i.e., if certain aims are overriding, the pluralist is allowed to privilege certain aims.

Because (on the reductivist view) the aims of science are hostage to the aims of scientists, the reductivist view fails. The actual aims of science will not license pluralism, nor monism, but rather nihilism. With t as the beginning and t' as the end of science, nothing satisfies the reductivist principle because scientists' aims are not uniform and their shared aims are not temporally stable.

In chapter 2, we saw the diversity of primary goals of geological scientists (as well as ways these goals influenced their reasoning). This situation is revealed both within and across other sciences as well: Many economists aim to predict or control economic systems; control of social social systems is almost never a goal of sociologists. Cognitive scientists aim to engineer intelligent behavior, but not all cognitive scientists have passing a Turing test as a primary goal: they may pursue the successful general (as opposed to anthropocentric) description of intelligence. Biologists typically seek explanatory results. Physicists are often content with accurate dynamics. Einstein, Podolsky and Rosen argued that quantum mechanics was incomplete, and implicitly suggested this is a shortcoming; Copenhagen was unperturbed.

Although the above cases describe what might be thought the typical aims of scientists from various scientific communities, it is important to recognize that scientists have had other primary goals: finishing a Ph.D. thesis, getting an NSF grant to avoid having to teach, playing with prisms, figuring out what Aristotle thought, edifying man by letting him more closely see the mind of God. Some science, such as medicine, seem to have highly practical aims in which truth is almost always subservient to practical outcomes.

We can divide the above cases into three kinds: those that show that within a community such candidate "scientific aims" as control of systems, prediction, accurate dynamics, and explanation, may be accepted by some while being rejected by others; those that show that from one field of science to another, the aims of scientists often differ; those that show that "unscientific aims" such as finishing theses, getting grants, human flourishing, and so forth, have been the primary goals of scientists. It is fair to say, given the diversity of all these sorts of aims, nothing satisfies x in the reductivist principle.

Some may not be convinced, and it will be difficult to convince them. Philosophers might imagine that scientists are not so different from philosophers as to have wholly distinct sorts of motivations, and philosophers, among other things, usually aim at truth. One might imagine, then, that scientists sometimes have priorities other than truth, even if truth is an aim. Such a philosopher needs to account for scientists who disavow truth as an aim. I wish now, however, to raise doubt about the relationship of progress to aims for the reductive view. The relationship between aims and progress is encapsulated in principle "(A)":

(A) if the aim of X is Y, then X makes progress when X achieves Y.[8]

A version of this principle is explicitly endorsed by Alexander Bird [Bir07b, 83] (see footnote 8) and is implicit in others. The first thing to note about (A) is that it is false in many cases: Journalism aims at truth; fishing aims at catches; archers aim at targets. Nevertheless, true newspaper articles, nets of salmon, and bull's-eyes are not progress for any of them. Successfully doing what one aims at is not generally sufficient for progress.[9] For present purposes, I am happy to concede that (A) holds for the particular case of science even if it does not hold generally.

Though I have already argued that science has no aims, I shall now argue that the aims that could plausibly result on the reductivist view are too inchoate for (A) to give a clear standard of progress.

A theory of scientific progress should state the relation that holds between stages of science when the difference between them is progressive. For example, if science progresses when it increases its labor pool, then the progressive relation is satisfied by pairs of stages in which the difference in manpower between the stages is positive. However, I will argue that on the reductive view, aims do not determine the progressive relation for the theory. Consequently, for the reductivist, either science does not progress or aims are unrelated to scientific progress.

The argument for this position is as follows:

---

[8]This principle is similar to the one that Alexander Bird [Bir07b, 83] calls "principle (A)," and it is where I get the name for the present principle. Bird's principle (A) says is "(A) if the aim of X is Y, then X makes progress when X achieves Y or *promotes the achievement of* Y." Mixing promoting progress and progress into the same bag may produce confusion and the notion of promotion was best left out of the concept of progress and instead left to the important role of explaining progress when it occurs. Nothing in the present argument depends on objecting to the notion that the idea of progress incorporates its promotion, Bird's principle may be substituted in place of (A) here.

[9]One worries that these cases are subject to worries like those about science raised in the present chapter, namely, that the aims of these activities are underdetermined by aims of their practitioners. However, the point of the present section is to raise concerns about the relationship between aims of science and scientific progress; these concerns are only made stronger if there is no such relationship.

(1) Plausible aims on the reductive view of aims of science are too inchoate to determine the progressive relation.
(2) Therefore, if aims of science determine the progressive relation, the reductive view is false. [1]
(3) If (A), then aims of science determine the progressive relation.
(4) Therefore, if (A) is true, the reductive view is false. [2, 3 by hypothetical syllogism]
(5) Therefore, either the reductive view is false or (A) is false. [4, by logical equivalence]

(3) is obvious, so the central question is about the first premise. Consider the view that science aims at truth. We can distinguish three types of aims at truth. First, a *specific* truth-aim is an aim to accept a particular proposition if and only if it is true. For example, one might aim at the truth of the speed of light in a vacuum; the aim is to accept a proposition that expresses the speed of light in a vacuum if and only if it is true. Second, a *general* truth-aim is an aim to accept truths, possibly only with regard to a specific domain. One may aim at truths generally or aim just at truths about light (while not aiming at other truth.) Some general aims will be *inchoate*: an aim is inchoate if and only if the aim and (A) underdetermine the progressive relation.[10] Aiming at maximizing truth is not inchoate: if one aims at maximizing truth, one progresses when one increases the number of truths one accepts. Aiming at truth, all other things with respect to truth being equal, is inchoate: when things regarding truth are not equal (e.g., if some truths are lost and others gained between two stages of science), nothing about progress is determined.[11]

The aim of truth[12] is inchoate in the following sense: the aim of truth can endorse

---

[10]The term 'inchoate' suggests that the aim is incomplete or not fully formed, which is exactly what I think that these aims amount to when they satisfy the technical definition here.

In what follows, some may come to reject the possibility of inchoate aims. Inchoate aims are the only candidate for shared aims of scientists; if there is no such thing, so much the worse for reductivism. My own view does not require the existence of inchoate aims.

[11]Inchoateness is different from being overridable. Those with an aim to maximize truth might have trouble when that aim conflicts with another aims. That does not make the aim of maximizing truth inchoate because considered solely with respect to truth, the aim to maximize is determinate. Aiming at truth, all other things with respect to truth being equal, does not tell us how truths should be valued against one another. In effect, the only condition under which that aim determines that something is progress is when, in matters of truths, it is costless.

[12]Hereafter, 'aim of truth' designates the general aim that a number of more specific aims can

multiple but incompatible progressive relations. Do successive stages, when progressive, show a net increase in the number of truths science endorses? Or does the successor stage, when progressive, accumulate truths, i.e., continue endorsing truths from its predecessor while increasing the total number of endorsed truths? Or does the successor stage need to show something deeper, such as implying in its theories more truths than its predecessor? These three question highlight three truth-aimed progressive relations. Moreover, these three relations can conflict. The possibility of conflict between net increase and accumulation is clear. The number of truths a theory implies can decrease while the number of truths a science endorses increases.[13] For example, if the number of observational and experimental truths increases but some accumulated truth conflicts with an extant theory, that theory may be rejected. Because a theory is rejected, fewer truths are implied in the theories science endorses. Nevertheless, the number of endorsed truths may increase because of the observational and experimental truths received.

This shows that the aim of truth is inchoate. The question that arises is whether scientists share a non-inchoate truth-aim. Insofar as the historical record reveals truth-aims among scientists, it will typically reveal specific truth aims. Scientists performing experiments, for example, will often have the particular truth-aim of determining whether some hypothesis is true. Moreover, individual scientists share few particular truth aims: insofar as they aim at particular truths, chemists aim at chemical ones, physicists at physical ones, geologists at geological ones, and so forth. The specific truth-aims of scientists are not shared. Moreover, sharing those specific aims would do little for a theory of progress, for we would get results similar to 'science progresses exactly when it discovers the speed of light.'

---

realize. Such specific aims include maximizing truth or maximizing the balance of truth over falsity. I shall use 'aim of maximizing truth', 'aim of maximizing the ratio of truths' and other suitable phrases to distinguish these more specific aims from the general aim of truth.

[13] One should read the present sense of 'imply' in a way that admits inductive prediction as an implication.

The historical record will no doubt reveal some scientists with a general non-inchoate truth-aim such as maximizing truths about light. However, it will also reveal more guarded sorts who seek an accurate account of light that avoids falsity. It will reveal those who sought a maximal ratio of truths to falsehoods. And it will reveal those who thought that theoretical implications of truths were especially important. This shows that general non-inchoate aims of scientists are not shared.

All that remains for scientists to share is the inchoate aim of truth. It is doubtful that scientists share the inchoate aim of truth, but if they did, it would be inadequate to determine a progressive relation. Thus concludes a defense of (1) with regard to the aim of truth: the only plausible shared truth-aim is the inchoate one that does not determine the progressive relation.

Mutatis mutandis, what has just been argued about the aim of truth is true of the aims of knowledge or puzzle-solutions, and for (*mutatis mutandis*) the same reasons. Explanation suffers likewise. (Consider: should scientists maximize the number of explanations they possess or seek to explain as much as possible within a single, unified framework? The diversity of philosophical accounts of explanation suggests that scientists have done many somewhat different things that may be regarded as explanatory.) Premise one is generally true: the only shared aims of scientists are inchoate.

Because of the diversity highlighted in the present chapter and chapter 2, I'm highly skeptical of the claim that scientists share aims; insofar as it can be shown that they do, such aims have little to do with the progress of science. Theorists seeking to ground progress in aims of science should seek somewhere other than the reductive view. The most plausible alternative takes aims to be an explanation of scientific norms.

4.1.2 Explanations of norms

Another account of the aim of science adopts the slogan "aims explain norms." According to this account, aims are things that justify or explain norms.[14] For example, it is a norm of driving in the United States that one drive on the right side of the road. The aim of the norm of driving on the road's right side is to solve a coordination problem so that we can enjoy cars free from the inefficiencies and dangers of people driving in whatever lane seems like a good idea at the time.

Hence, insofar as there are norms of science, one might want to explain or justify those norms by reference to an aim.[15] Moreover, we certainly think that there is such a thing as being unscientific, and this is usually a normative notion. We think that there are scientific methods that prescribe ways of substantiating and testing hypotheses, refuting theories, and so forth. The strategy under consideration is thus: find those aims that best explain or justify the norms of scientific activity; those are the aims of science.

An initial and obvious problem confronts the explanatory view: there is no agreed upon set of norms of scientific practice. Some might thus infer that seeking the aims of science in its norms is a hopeless task. Obviously, I'm circumspect about the view that there are clear norms of scientific practice. I have thus far advocated a view according to which the diversity of scientists regarding methodological standards is profitable. In light of this, I'm unlikely to be convinced that the alleged explanandum for explanatory aims is real; nevertheless, I shall give some time to the problems that I think arise even if we admit that the norms of scientific practice are stable across times, sciences, and scientists. Though the details of various kinds of scientific reasoning

---

[14]This account needn't be a *general* account of aims, though it certainly works well for many cases; here I merely mean to illustrate the approach with examples and articulate the view as it applies to aims of science.

[15]There is obviously quite a difference between explaining and justifying. However, none of my criticism of the idea that aims explain (or justify) norms shall turn especially on the difference. The problem will be that norms underdetermine aims regardless of whether one looks for justificatory or explanatory aims.

are controversial, let us assume that there are fairly well agreed upon standards of inductive evidence and theoretical virtues. Scientists appeal to correct predictions of their theories as the empirical evidence. They can also appeal to coherence with other confirmed theories as empirical evidence. Furthermore, there are "superempirical" virtues of theory choice, such as simplicity, that scientists appeal to. Let us allow these traditional thoughts about scientific practice to form an explanandum for aims that explain norms. Indeed, I seem to be in the minority in questioning whether such norms are real.

Despite broad agreement about scientific norms (my own dissent withstanding), there is little agreement about aims, either among the philosophers that study the matter or the scientists that practice it. Larry Laudan [Lau84, 43–50] raises an important point in this context, which he calls the covariance fallacy. That fallacy is assuming that if scientists agree (or disagree) about axiological points, they agree (or disagree) about factual points, methodological points or both; it is "the covariance fallacy" because it assumes covariance of methodological, factual and axiological attitudes among scientists. And indeed, Laudan contends that scientists often agree about methods while disagreeing about the justification or explanation of those methods. Conversely, they may agree about aims while disagreeing about methods. This is not good news for the view that aims explain norms. Nor is another, and quite similar fact: though philosophers are in fairly widespread agreement about the norms of scientific practice, there is little agreement in the debate between instrumentalism, empiricism and realism. To take a well-known example, van Fraassen agrees with realists that scientists appeal to superempirical virtues, but he disagrees with realists about the point and substance of such appeals.

A fundamental problem for the view that aims explain norms is that a particular norm can be followed in service of different aims. Given that one has certain aims, there may be norms to follow; however, given a set of norms to follow, one needn't have some particular aim. Truth, prediction, understanding and puzzle-solving power can each be offered to explain such norms as we find in science. The norms of science underdetermine its aims.[16]

For those not convinced that aims equally well explain the collection of scientific norms, there is a further problem for aims explaining norms: insofar as we find aims to explain norms, they will be inchoate aims. The argument (1–5) above will, *mutatis mutandis*, apply to the view that aims explain norms as well.

It is a well-known fact that the norms of science discussed above may conflict. Coherence and unification, for example, are two norms of theory choice in science. A coherent theory fits well with other accepted theory; a unifying theory collects diverse phenomena in a single account. A classic example is the early debate between the Copernican and Ptolemaic models of the solar system. One merit of the Copernican theory is that it explained many phenomena (e.g., retrograde motion) as a built-in feature of the geometry of the solar system. However, the Copernican theory conflicted with the 16th century physics. The coherence norm is arguably a matter of a kind of risk aversion, avoiding the loss of truth.[17] The unification norm is arguably a matter of maximizing the built-in predictions of one's theory. These two easily come into conflict, for the theory that collects diverse phenomena may require rejecting some results of the body of accepted science. Although truth is related to each of these justifications of the norm, only an inchoate truth-aim that can provide all these justifications. Consequently, even if the best explanation of the norms of science is a truth-aim, it is the inchoate aim of truth that does this explanation. Since such an aim determines no progressive relation, it would have little to do with scientific progress.

---

[16]Alexander Bird [Bir07b] has recently offered truth, knowledge and puzzle-solving power as the historical candidates for the target of progress. Their explicit inclusion here is exemplary, not exhaustive.

[17]In other cases, we think that aims other than those considered here best justify these norms. This would just be grist for my mill: if the very same norms are justified by one aim in one context and another aim in a different context, that would be excellent evidence that norms underdetermine aims.

Epistemological norms are not the only norms of science; sociological norms of science are another potential explanandum if aims explain norms. Sociological norms of science cover an array of practices in science. They regulate practices of attribution, authority, and publication. They govern the distribution of resources science has to allocate. Indeed, many epistemic norms of science are sociological in the sense that there is a public requirement of adhering to those norms. Trends in the philosophy of science since Kuhn have emphasized the degree to which science is a social activity that depends upon the interaction of many individuals. Realist accounts that have incorporated such ideas were slower to emerge than the anti-realist versions; those accounts emphasize that the success of science is highly dependent on the ways in which science coordinates individual activity. Thus, from the fact that we are explaining something sociological rather than epistemological, it should not be inferred that the results will be anti-realist in character.

The notion of a sociological norm needs some clarification. In [Mer42], Merton used the term 'norm' for his four norms of scientific practice: communism, disinterestedness, organized skepticism, and universalism. These norms were intended to explain the development of scientific communities; the power of the norms to do so, i.e., the fact that scientific communities adhere to these norms, Merton [Mer57] partially explained with a system of reward. According to Merton, the rewards of credit and priority help to keep scientists, for the most part, behaving according to the four norms. In my sense of "norm," however, I intend to include the system of rewarding scientists as a norm of scientific practice.

In my sense, norms are permissions and restrictions expressible with "ought" or "may" statements. For example, "all other things being equal, one ought to select the simplest theory" expresses an Occam's razor principle that has been alleged to be a norm of theory choice in science.[18] Another norm of science is expressible with

---

[18] I make no claim here about the point of such a norm. The present formulation may oversimplify the requirement for simple theories that is a scientific norm.

"one ought to acknowledge the originator of a scientific idea that one uses." Another is "one may freely use the ideas of others to develop further scientific ideas." A norm is sociological when it involves the way a scientific community works as opposed to merely the way an individual works. (Note that a sociological norm may thus also be an epistemic one when it involves community level practices that are epistemic in nature, such as offering justification to others.)

With this in hand, let's consider a few cases of sociological norms and see whether they are best explained via an appeal to an aim. The array of sociological norms of science is vast, and as with epistemic norms, we have no uniform agreement about what they are. However, by considering cases, the degree to which norms underdetermine aims becomes salient. The present case is not an artificial one but drawn from the developed literature on sociological norms of science. The present argument will show that in that case, the norms underdetermine the aims of science. It places a strong burden of proof on the advocate of the idea that aims explain norms to show that any norms determine the aims of science.

One of Kitcher's norms of science [Kit93, chapter 8][Kit90] is that resources should be allocated to scientists in proportion to their contributions to successful research projects. When the debate between two rival research projects closes, the spoils go the victors. The spoils will include prestige, grant opportunities, and tenure track positions. The result of such a norm is that scientists are invested in the success of their research projects and in the failure of their rivals'. Consequently, scientists have an incentive to behave in ways that promote their own success and promote the failure of rivals. Scientists have incentives to be critical of rival research because this undermines its chance of success. Scientists have incentives to respond to criticism of their own work because it undermines their chance of success. As a results, the community exposes the faults of research projects but it also repairs them, and scientists have a reason to do the detailed work that may be essential to defeating or saving a research project. Scientists have incentives to check the research of others that they rely upon because if that research is faulty, its faults may contaminate the scientist's results.[19] This would sound like a system ripe for malfeasance, a system ready to encourage dishonest criticism for the sake of a pet theory. However, if we add to this Merton's observation [Mer57] that scientists are not penalized for honest failed work, except in opportunity costs, but lose their professional license for engaging in fraudulent work, we see that scientists have an incentive to make their criticisms honest and genuine.

We can sum up the result of the norms above by saying that sociological norms of science produce a critical community. But now the point raised against epistemic norms returns: the aim of truth, or knowledge, or predictive success, or instrumental usefulness—take whichever of these you like—none seems obviously a better explanation or justification of having a critical community than the others. Norms underdetermine aims. Moreover, insofar as they determine aims, those aims would be inchoate, and so would underdetermine the conditions of scientific progress.[20]

4.1.3 Vague Aims

One possibility that I haven't considered is that the aims of science are vague. Rather than picking out some precise progressive relation, the aims pick out a vague entity similar to all of these. The vague aim of science might be identified with a collection of precise aims and a specification of progressive relations. Progress in the sense of any one of these precise progressive relations would be partial progress but progress would not demand any particular one of these. Regress would be partial progress in reverse, i.e. if the transition from A to B is partially progressive, then a transition in

---

[19] It is an awfully generous person who donates his time to retesting another person's hypothesis for its own sake. Little credit accrues to recheckers. However, if that work can used for further purposes, individuals have a reason to check it because they may get credit for something else.

[20] More anti-realist accounts of sociological norms have tried to show that the norms of science determinately rule out realist goals such as truth or knowledge as a aims of science. However, I think such works have been far too sanguine in assuming the epistemic impotence of what Kitcher [Kit93, especially Chapter 8] calls "epistemically sullied" agents. To summarize Kitcher's arguments, he shows that communities with certain sorts of structures can operate effectively in spite of and even because of individuals with non-epistemic aims.

the opposite direction, from B to A, is partially regressive. Science determinately progresses when it partially progresses without partially regressing. Science completely progresses when it partially progresses with respect to every possibility of partial progress.

As an example, science might have the vague aim of truth, where this is aim is constituted by increasing truth, decreasing falsehood and improving the balance among them. The transition from A to B partially progresses regarding this vague aim of truth if (1) B has more truth than A, (2) B has less falsehood than A, or (3) the ratio of truths to falsehoods in B is greater than in A. The transition from A to B *partially regressive* regarding this vague aim of truth if (1′) A has more truth than B, (2′) A has less falsehood than B or (3′) the ratio of truths to falsehoods in A is greater than in B. A transition is *determinately progress* when it is partial progress but not partial regress; for example, if (1) occurs but neither (2′) nor (3′) occurs, there is determinate progress. The transition from B to A is *completely progressive* if all of (1), (2) and (3) are satisfied.

I don't see why this is anything more than a polished semantics on a pluralist view of progress. Of course, if one is a pluralist (I am), one might find the semantics helpful, especially perhaps in diagnosing certain somewhat confusing discussions with the word 'progress' in them. But I don't see a special *theoretical* advantage to introducing this semantics within the theory of progress.[21] However, the central issue for vague aims is to specify how and why some particular vague aim becomes the aim of science. Vague aims may help to obviate inchoate aims, but that doesn't make the problem of grounding aims easier: what facts determine that a vague aim of truth rather than

---

[21]Moreover, as regards real aims of science, a problem of higher-order vagueness arises: given a particular choice of precise aims that constitute the vague aim of science, there is a subtly distinct vague aim which adds or removes some precise aim to get a subtly different vague aim. The problem of saying which aim science has simply repeats itself for the possible vague ends of science in a mirror of the standard problem of higher-order vagueness. Where we previously wished to know which precise aim was the aim of science, we now wish to know which vague aim is the aim of science. (If we understand these vague aims as models of science rather than as descriptions, I see some potential theoretical advantage here, but it seems semantic rather than substantive.)

a vague aim of knowledge is the aim of science? Following the discussion above, we have two broad proposals: scientists share vague aims; vague aims explain norms. I don't see how making the aims vague does anything to obviate the problems of underdetermination we raised before.

In addition to the two broad proposals involving vague aims above, there is a third, new proposal arises in the context of vague aims. This proposal is similar to reductivism; although scientists don't share aims, their aims are similar, and this gives rise to a vague community aim constituted of their individual aims. Imagine that three different scientists compose a scientific community. Scientist A has the aim of increasing the total number of truths within their theory. Scientist B has the aim of reducing falsity withing their theory. Scientist C has the aim of increasing the ratio of truths to falsehoods. For simplicity, let's call these aims a, b, and c after their respective havers. There is no shared aim among these scientists. However, a philosophical theory might tell us that the community has a vague aim of truth because each of these scientists has a more or less truth directed aim. This vague aim will have the relation to progress described above: when a is achieved but neither b nor c is, there is determinate progress regarding a but not complete progress; when all are achieved, there is complete progress; when some are achieved but others hindered, there is partial progress and partial regress, and so forth.

The small, toy community used to explicate the idea that underlies this third proposal misleadingly portrays the constitution of community aims as a simple affair. But with actual science, one is dealing with hundreds or thousands of people. Some of their aims may be semantically contrary and others contrary in practice if not in principle. Scientific communities may contain, for example, individuals seeking to articulate a theory of unobservable entities that perform explanatory functions in a wide range of contexts while other seek to purge science of metaphysical excesses— unobservable entities being an exemplary case of alleged excess. The third account has some considerable, difficult work in saying when and why particular aims of scientists are included in the community aim.

The third account account has a curious implication: neither B nor C should regard promotion of a as significant, yet according to the theory, there is determinate progress when a is achieved. I won't say that there's something totally unacceptable about the conclusion. It is, however, odd. Further oddity arises when we consider the relation between this vague aim and norms. There's a natural story to tell about which norms apply to A: they're the norms that promote a.[22] Moreover, those norms apply because A aims at a. But the story of the vague aim is that those norms apply because the community has a vague truth aim. While some of those will no doubt promote a the explanatory story seems to get it wrong; indeed, even if exactly the same norms followed from each aim, the story seems wrong. A's aim of a—not the community's vague truth aim—explains why A should follow the norms that he should.

So, although the semantics of an inchoate aim can be cashed out in terms of a vague aim as I have described, the picture of science that results seems mistaken. The introduction of vague aims may offer a level of semantic clarity and may fit better with the facts of diversity in scientific communities than precise aims. However, the ultimate relation between aims, norms and progress that results from vagues aims is in no way superior to the account with precise aims that has already been rejected.

4.1.4 Brute Facts?

A final strategy remains, as an act of desperation, to the theorist who insists that science aims. This strategy is just that: insist that science aims. The aims of science are brute facts about it that cannot be reduced to other facts about science, nor do

---

[22]The exact details here are, of course, subtle. The present construal is externalist; those with internalist leanings will tend to say that A should follows norms which by his lights promote a. The exact relationship between aims and norms is a matter of just philosophical attention. But neither internalists nor externalists will characterize the norms that apply to A in terms of b or c, and so the point here stands regardless of leanings in debates about externalism.

they serve to explain norms.

Such a theory of the aims of science has little to recommend it. The principle problem is a dilemma: the view dissolves either into unacceptable table-pounding about the particular aims of science or into questionable insistence that there are aims coupled with skepticism about what the aims are. Table-pounding can be the only result for this view where disagreement about aims arises. The view that the brute facts about aims of science are accessible via facts about aims of scientists or explanations of the norms of science is ruled out by the considerations above. Any identification of the aims of science is thus unprincipled, and debates about them will be mere table-pounding. If brute facts are unknown, brute facts engender skepticism: science aims, though at what we cannot know.

4.1.5 The Standard Realist Aim

Up to this point, I have argued that nothing grounds claims about aims of science, and, therefore, that science has none. In this section I consider directly whether the standard realist aim succeeds in describing scientific activity and providing an evaluative standard for that activity. The standard aim of science according to scientific realists is to explain and predict the natural world. Of course, I will argue that science does not have explanatory or predictive aims. Before proceeding, I should emphasize that not aiming at something is not to deny the possibility of progressing toward that thing. To progress is to improve more or less monotonically regarding something (see §1.2); science may improve in both explanatory and predictive power without *aiming* to do so.[23]

If explanation and prediction are the aims of science, then "explanatory" and

---

[23]Other objections to the notion of increasing explanatory and predictive power will not be considered here. The most prominent of these is van Fraassen's [van80] issue of pragmatics of explanation. However, I suspect that his issue is a bit of a red herring: if he is right, we cannot attribute explanatory power to theories, but we might nevertheless claim that scientific communities improve their answers to why questions.

"predictive" will typically seem like the a better description of individual sciences than alternative descriptions of their aims, and activity within those sciences will typically seem organized (whether individually or communally) by that aim. But the explanatory and predictive account of the aim of medicine hardly seems like a better account of medicine's aim than aims of the elimination of disease and the promotion of health. Likewise, prediction in economics often seems subservient to practical decisions that economics is intended to inform. Does the list of titles on oxygen measurement in §3.4 suggest that scientific work on oxygen is principally explanatory?

Such observations are sometimes rebutted with appeals to a distinction between pure and applied science: we apply sciences to achieve our practical ends, but we theorize to explain and predict. Any of the sciences may be applied, but to point to their applications as evidence that they are not theoretical ignores the two kinds of scientific work. *Pure* science aims to explain and predict the natural world, pure science can be assessed by its contribution to those aims, and scientist qua theorist can be assessed by looking to whether her behavior conduces to achieving them.

In offering the distinction between pure and applied science, we must be careful not to render the explanatory and predictive aim of science vacuous by saying that science aims to explain and predict when scientists aim to explain and predict, for it will be unsurprising to find that, when scientists aim to explain and predict, their activity is organized around explanation and prediction, and it will be perfectly ordinary to evaluate those scientists with respect to *their* aims. However, if science aims to explain and predict, then there should be cases when scientific work should be measured against the standard of promoting those aims regardless of the aims of scientists; to draw the line between pure and applied science solely in terms of scientists' intentions will not say where this line is.

On a certain (naïve) conception of science according to which applied science is merely applying pure science, one might draw this line by saying that science is applied when it merely uses science developed with the aim of explanation and prediction for other purposes. But few cases of applied science are like that; while science developed with theoretical aims often plays a role in applied science, applied science must frequently develop it's own apparatus to achieve its practical ends—applied science is not *merely* the application of theoretical science. Moreover, much theoretical science derives impetus from practical ends, even if the aims of scientists involved are theoretical. The *practical* significance of super conductivity, for example, is certainly part of the reason that it is the subject of much *theoretcial* work.

The second test of explanatory and predictive aims is to say when these aims provide evaluative criteria for scientific work despite the alternative aims of scientists who produce the work in question. A great deal of obviously scientific work (consider the titles on oxygen from §3.4) does not obviously contribute to these aims. Does that work thereby become non-scientific? Does it become unscientific? The answer would seem to be "no." For these paper, an important counter-factual conditional emerges: if these works did not contribute to explanation or prediction, they would nevertheless be scientific. Moreover, there has been a great deal of work done on scientific problems where that conditional is not counter-factual: past scientific work of a specialized nature ("normal science") that belongs to research programs that are now extinct does not cease to be scientific. At the turn of the twentieth century, mechanics investigated the properties of unusual tops (like the child's toy). But these investigations have largely died because they were classical Newtonian investigations.[24] These investigations never yielded substantive explanatory or predictive results by any present standard. Can we thus call them unscientific? Similar things could be said about vast amounts of scientific research within past scientific "paradigms."

For these reasons, I conclude that science does not aims at explanation or prediction.

---

[24] I owe the example to Shaughan Lavine from conversation.

4.2 Reconsidering Aims of Science

The chapter has focused on potential accounts of aims of science and shown that they fail. If none of these accounts can succeed, why have so many philosophers claimed that science aims? In this final section I want to consider what I take to be the most plausible positive argument for supposing that science has aims.

The argument that I think has tempted some into thinking about science as having aims claims that a coherent picture of science requires us to suppose that science aims even if we cannot say what its aims are. The argument is as follows: Either science has aims or scientific norms are inexplicable and their enforcement is arbitrary. Without aims, norms are purposeless, and purposeless enforcements of norms are arbitrary. However, because the enforcement of scientific norms is not arbitrary, the norms are explicable. Hence, science aims. The alleged theoretical advantage of aims is that they avoid a mistaken picture of science with purposeless, arbitrarily enforced and inexplicable norms.

That argument certainly is tempting, and I suspect it's appeal has tacitly led many to suppose that science must have aims. But the appeal is illusory. It is sufficient to explain the local, individual enforcements of norms; a further demand to explain a global, community-level fact that science enforces particular norms is not necessary. Take, for example, the norm that science ought to expel frauds. The argument above supposes that this global community fact needs an explanation in terms of aims of science. However, ultimately, the local behavior of individual scientists gives rise to expulsion; if instances of that behavior can be explained without appeal to an aim, aims are unnecessary to explaining the norm. What explains the community-level fact is the local behavior of individual scientists. Moreover, some norms of science are enforced because norms are instrumental to achieving individual aims regardless of what those aims are.[25] Scientists rely on the work of other scientists; it is exceedingly

---

[25]It's unlikely that any aim whatsoever can be supported by certain norms; the point is that myr-

rare to find individual scientists who can accomplish their goals without relying on the work of others. Consequently, individual scientists have a reason to enforce norms against fraud. However, that fact does not need to stem from some shared aims, but rather the instrumental utility of a reliable community, for a reliable peer group may serve scientists with contrary aims.

The argument for aims is correct in demanding an explanation of the norms of science. But it is mistaken in assuming that some community-level fact (one of having an aim) is essential to such an explanation. Instead of community aims to explain community norms, we appeal to lower level facts of individual behavior and motivation. Those facts serve to explain the phenomena without delivering community aims.

---

iad aims of individual scientists, even aims contrary to one another, can be supported by community norms and hence scientists individually have their reasons for supporting them.

CHAPTER 5

KNOWLEDGE AND SCIENTIFIC DEVELOPMENT

Claims that science is knowledge are widespread. They appear in diverse places, from throw-away comments on the jackets of philosophy books to academic papers asserting that it is the target of scientific progress and the very goal of science [Bir07b]. But the relationship between science and knowledge needs clarification: Science is the product of scientific communities, and knowledge is a distinguished subset of token belief; science is a community achievement, knowledge is an achievement of believers. Whether something is science or knowledge depends upon how it was produced, but, whereas there is only one scientific community, there are many believers and it is a separate question for each believer whether she knows what she believes. Consequently, investigation of individual beliefs may yield diverse verdicts regarding knowledge, but there is only one community to assess. If the product of the scientific community is knowledge (or, at least, in many special cases it is), the question arises: what is the belief of the community (or whose belief is the pertinent one) and how do we assess its justification, that we may call this community achievement knowledge?

The thesis of this chapter is that the concept of knowledge is inadequate for description of scientific development. This is because description of scientific development in terms of knowledge is incomplete, adding knowledge to an otherwise complete description adds nothing, and attempts to describe scientific progress in terms of knowledge obfuscate important features of scientific development.

In arguing this thesis I am opposing Alexander Bird, who has argued that knowledge is "the concept we need to understand what scientific progress is." [Bir07b, 64] Bird calls this position the epistemic conception of scientific progress. Bird's first argument for the epistemic conception of progress derives from his claim that belief aims at knowledge; I argue against this claim in §5.1. In §5.2, I argue for the main thesis of this chapter, that the concept of knowledge fails to successfully describe scientific development. In §5.3, I turn to another argument of Bird's for the epistemic conception of scientific progress.

Allow me to offer a provisional definition of the concept of knowledge. Knowledge is a hotly debated philosophical concept, and in giving this definition, my goal is to encompass as much as possible shared ideas about knowledge.[1] My hope is to be helpfully vague by offering an uncontroversial starting point for discussion, from which a better conception of knowledge can be refined. Knowledge is a subspecies of true belief, and what differentiates knowledge from mere true belief depends upon the process by which the belief was formed and maintained. I follow recent philosophical tradition and call any process sufficient to make a true belief knowledge *warrant*. Being warranted is different, at least conceptually, from being justified; one is *justified* exactly if the way one's belief is formed supports that belief (typically, as a matter of having related that belief to evidence for it.) (Note that having formed a belief in such a way is different from possessing evidence which allows one to form a belief in such a way.) Which processes are justifying is a complex matter; clearly, haphazard guessing and wishful thinking aren't. On the other hand, it seems that one may use evidence to support belief. Suppose that 9 out of 10 pitchers with a 97 mile per hour fastball require ligament replacement surgery ("Tommy John" surgery), and that Stephen Strasburg throws 97. There's an intuitive sense in which, all other things being equal, these two facts would support the belief that Strasburg will require Tommy John surgery. If I support my belief on this basis, I am justified in believing that Strasburg will require ligament replacement surgery. Exactly what is required for me to support my belief is a controversial matter. I discuss more precise accounts of justification and warrant below. Being justified is not only a matter of how one forms

---

[1] Pryor [Pry01] is an excellent source on the subject of recent epistemology and has influenced the present discussion.

beliefs, but how one maintains them in light of further reasoning and experience; for expository convenience, I shall call the way in which a belief is formed and maintained a 'process of believing.' For the present discussion, I will take it that, barring special considerations, justification is a necessary condition of warrant.

A much less discussed feature of knowledge, but important to the case at hand, is this: in the first instance, all knowledge is knowledge for someone. Allow me to clarify. In the first instance, it does not make sense to say that 'Some swans are black' is knowledge *simpliciter*. Rather, 'some swans are black' is knowledge for some individuals but not for others. This follows from the fact that whether a token belief is knowledge depends on the process of believing relevant to it; since, presumably, any proposition may be believed without warrant, it follows that no proposition is knowledge without being known by someone, and that proposition may not be known by everyone who believes it. The qualifier 'in the first instance' is meant to indicate that there might be ways to count a proposition as knowledge while it "belongs to no one" or perhaps is not, strictly speaking, a belief. In the present context, it is essential that something may count as knowledge in some such secondary, derivative sense because the content of science is not, strictly speaking, any particular token belief. This will be important below.

5.1 The Aim of Belief

One of Bird's arguments for the epistemic conception of scientific progress depends on the claim that belief aims at knowledge. (The view that belief aims at knowledge originates with Timothy Williamson [Wil00].) I disagree with Bird's view that belief aims at knowledge; indeed, I disagree that belief has any aim at all. I begin my discussion of the epistemic conception of scientific progress by criticizing the view that belief aims at knowledge.

In arguing against the claim that belief has an aim, I am not opposing the claim that token beliefs have aims. When an individual agent forms beliefs through conscious direction, it is likely that she did so to satisfy a particular goal of hers. In such a case, it is arguable that the aim of that belief is to satisfy that goal or to assist in satisfying that goal. I am neither endorsing nor rejecting that token beliefs aim in these circumstances, nor that token beliefs could aim in some other way. The view that I reject, and the one that Bird and Williamson endorse, is that all believing is, *ipso facto*, aiming to know.

Bird articulates the idea that belief aims at knowledge by appealing to the function of the capacity to believe [Bir10][Bir07a, 94]. According to Bird, cognitive capacities, like anatomical organs, have functions, and the aim of the capacity is to fulfill its function. The function of the capacity to believe is to produce knowledge and make it available to other cognitive systems.

Let us explore this analogy between cognitive capacities and anatomical organs. The view that anatomical organs have aims fits well with functioning we typically observe in them. Prominent factors in judgments about the functions of anatomical organs include what anatomical organs do in ordinary functioning and how that ordinary functioning is related to an organism's survival. The lungs, for example, ordinarily absorb oxygen into the blood stream and expel carbon dioxide from the blood stream. When the ordinary functioning of the lungs is prevented, suffocation results. Our natural conclusion is that the function of the lungs is to provide oxygen for respiration and expel the waste of respiration. This natural conclusion could be challenged; I don't claim that this is the only account of the function of the lungs that we could give, nor that we must draw that conclusion that the lungs have a function. However, if the lungs did not characteristically exhibit this behavior, it would be odd to assign them this function. In short, if an organ has a function, it characteristically exhibits behavior associated with that function.

This is problematic for Bird's view because belief does not characteristically exhibit behavior associated with knowing. There are two cases of belief that we should consider in this context. The first are automatically formed beliefs that result from cognitive processes outside our conscious direction. The second are those consciously directed beliefs that result from cognitive processes under our direction.[2] By far, the majority of our beliefs are of the automatic, undirected variety. Insofar as belief is an important part of navigating our world, consciously formed beliefs are inadequate to the task because we posses far too few of them to guide our behavior, and conscious formation of belief is too slow for efficient use in many contexts. Consider, for example, an ordinary conversation in which you attempt to consciously regulate every belief you form on the basis of the utterances of the people you are talking with; it would be almost impossible to carry on a conversation if this happened. However, psychological evidence suggests that automatically formed beliefs come from a range of process that don't resemble norms of good epistemic reasoning. The studies of Kahneman and Tversky, for example, show a broad range of human behavior that seems, by traditional lights, irrational. The bulk of our beliefs are automatically formed, but many of the processes that form them are non-justifying. They result from heuristics whose roles seems to be efficiency rather than justification. (As an example, consider the Monty Hall problem: a contestant in a game show is asked to guess which door the prize is behind. Once she guesses, she is told that it is not behind one of the doors she did not guess, and she is then given the chance to change her mind. It is demonstrable that given her new information, she should change her mind. Nevertheless, in psychological studies, very few people change their guess in response to the new information.) Consequently, automatically formed beliefs don't seem to aim at knowing because many of them are formed by processes that are not characteristically justificatory.

Automatically formed beliefs are the bulk of our beliefs, and, thus, belief in gen-

---

[2] I take it that some cognitive processes are never under our direction, some are always under our direction, and some can be directed by us and will also operate independently. I may spontaneously remember that I need to buy milk today, but I may also probe my memory for the things I need to get at the store.

eral does not aim at knowledge. However, because scientists' beliefs are (arguably) consciously formed, it is important to consider separately whether consciously formed beliefs aim at knowing. Once again, contrasting belief with similar cases is instructive. The aim of other behaviors is inherited from my goals, and it would be unusual if belief were different.[3] Belief seems subject to goal-relative evaluation. Suppose for example you are offered a bet of ten dollars with even odds that Babe Ruth allowed the fewest runs per inning of any American League pitcher in 1917. You quickly reason the because pitchers are rarely even average hitters (much less great ones) and Ruth was a great hitter, it is highly unlikely that he was a pitcher, much less an excellent one. On this basis, you accept the bet.

In accepting the bet, your cognitive state is not merely one in which you think a certain action is practical. It seems that you believe that Ruth wasn't the best pitcher in 1917; you have not merely reasoned that the expected utility of taking the bet is high. There are many cases in which you will accept bets without believing in the bet (because you have calculated the utility of the bet in a certain way), but this is not one of those. Your confidence is not, so to speak, one-hundred percent, but you think your chain of reasoning is strong and you are certainly willing to act on your belief.

You would win the bet; Eddie Cicotte, not Babe Ruth, led the American League in ERA in 1917. Nevertheless, it is certainly arguable that you don't know that Ruth wasn't the ERA leader in 1917. The reason is that Ruth was 7th among 36 qualified pitchers and, in 1916, Ruth was the ERA leader. Your principle that pitchers aren't good hitters doesn't apply to Ruth, who was a pitcher the first four years of his career until the Yankees decided that he would be more valuable if he were a hitter every day.[4] Nevertheless, I find nothing defective in your belief that Ruth was not the ERA

---

[3]I find the locution of behaviors aiming somewhat unfortunate and prefer to say that agents aim at things and behave in ways to accomplish their aims, but the point seems mostly terminological in this context.

[4]The physical demands of pitching require that players take days off after each game, so full-time

leader in 1917, nor in your process of belief that supports it. It seems well-reasoned and comports with your goals of deciding whether to accept this bet.

Suppose, however, that we change the example by changing your goals. Instead of trying to make a bet, you are developing an avid interest in baseball. When there's no baseball to watch, you spend some of your free time learning about the history of the sport. At some point, you encounter the question, "Did Babe Ruth lead the American League in ERA in 1917?" Our assessment of your previous believing process changes in this case. As someone whose goals specifically involve the history of baseball, it is tempting to say that you should be more circumspect in your believing process. Indeed, precisely because it would be an exception to the rule that pitchers are not good hitters, it seems you should investigate the question (when you get the chance) and withhold your belief while investigation is pending. This question is especially interesting to you, not only because it would be an exception to an otherwise good rule, but because this particular possible exception involves one of the luminaries of the game. Resting content with the simple reasoning process encountered previously seems inadequate in the present case.[5]

This suggests an alternative account of the function of belief: it is to provide representations (of a certain sort) for the regulation of action and cognition in accordance with the goals of the agent. If this is correct, the agent's goals provide the principle source of evaluative criteria for beliefs. Regardless of whether this is correct, the present two cases tell against knowledge as the aim of belief. By varying factors involved with the agent's interest in and goals with believing, we discover different

---

pitchers play fewer games than a full time hitters, who do not need regular days off.

[5]Some recent views in epistemology, relevant alternatives theories, suggest that whether or not one is justified depends on whether one has eliminated all relevant alternatives. For example, suppose that you are looking at a zoo exhibit of African animals. In order to know that what you are seeing is a gazelle, you must be able to eliminate the relevant alternative that it is an antelope, but you need not eliminate the alternative that it is a carefully disguised donkey, because that is an irrelevant alternative. Such views do not, however, present a challenge to the present argument, for in each case there are two alternatives, Babe Ruth was the ERA leader and someone else was the ERA leader; no new possibilities exist for me to eliminate as a result of changing goals, so these changes in goals cannot amount to changing the class of relevant alternatives.

grounds for assessments. This produces a direct counterexample to knowledge as the aim of belief. Moreover, it suggests that believing is not, *ipso facto*, aiming at anything, but rather that the aim of particular beliefs is dictated by our aims.[6]

5.2 Knowledge and Scientific Development

This section argues that the concept of knowledge does not typically apply to the products of the scientific community, i.e., to science. I emphasize the fact that knowledge is a path dependent state and that the typical development of scientific agreement is not analogous to the path that individual knowledge takes; in particular, justification is typically a feature of warranted belief, but scientific communities are not justified in anything like the individual way. Consequently, scientific agreements are not warranted and (consequently) not knowledge.[7]

If we wish to describe scientific progress in terms of knowledge, we need to say what it is for science to be knowledge. In the first instance, all knowledge is knowledge

---

[6]Two points here: First, in conversation, Richard Healey objects that I have just said what belief aims at, viz., the regulation of cognition and action in accordance with goals. It seems wrong to me to say that the believing is *ipso facto* aiming to regulate cognition and action: regulation of cognition and action are pre-conditions of achieving one's goals, not goals themselves.

Second, the view that belief aims at knowledge explains an alleged norm of believing, namely, *believe only truths that your evidence favors*, and I suspect that this is part of the motivation for accepting it. This norm produces a means to identify defects in cognitive states, and to criticize agents on the basis of those defects. Given this norm, it follows that scientists' beliefs are criticizable, and hence an agreement among them is, unless those beliefs are held on the basis of evidence. However, if scientists ought to believe only if they have sufficient evidence, then scientists ought to conform to the principle *differential knowledge*; see page 144.

As explicitly stated, the norm *believe only those truths which your evidence favors* is incorrect. According to this norm, our beliefs should be responsive to our total body of evidence. However, our beliefs should be responsive to our (conscious and unconscious) reasoning. That is, beliefs should be responsive to evidence as we reason about it. (The best work I know on this subject is Pollock and Cruz [PC99, ch. 5].) Are there norms for what we should and should not reason about? Perhaps there are, but they will make reference to goals of agents.

[7]A different argument that science is not knowledge appeals to the fact that a number of products of science are not representations and thus not even candidates to be believed; therefore, they cannot be knowledge. However, whereas the substantial emphasis of this dissertation has been upon progress manifest in scientific representations, I shall bracket these considerations (to which I am sympathetic), and focus on whether knowledge is well-suited to description of scientific representations and to their development.

for someone, so if science is knowledge then we must ask "for whom?" Science is the agreement of a scientific community. Indeed, the need to say how the product of science is related to knowledge becomes clear once we consider that the product is not a belief. It is natural to ask "what is the belief of the relevant scientific community?" The answer, of course, is the agreement of the community. Under what conditions is the agreement knowledge?

The agreement of a community is like a belief in that the agreement will need to be true and warranted to be knowledge. Truth of agreement presents no special theoretical problem. To be warranted, the agreement needs to be justified. Unlike truth, group justification presents special problems. What is the community's justification of their shared belief? It is dialectically helpful to begin with a naive view of science as knowledge which says that an agreement is justified if each member of the community shares a justification for the agreement, that is, it is justified if, in addition to agreeing about the representation in question, they also agree about a justification for the representation.

This is one way to define knowledge for a group, but it's not the way that science develops. As we have seen in chapter 2, scientific agreements develop by convergence. The suggestion of the naive view for how an agreement is knowledge requires consensus, and without a consensus, nothing would count as justified. If a justified agreement is one for which there is a shared justification, few scientific agreements are justified. (One *could* respond to this with a kind of skepticism, and claim that science might have produced knowledge but does not because it produces no justifications— so much the worse for science, but this is a tepid skepticism, since many people might nevertheless know topics of scientific agreement.) The naive view fails because it identifies warrant with shared justification, and shared justification is consensus agreement. However, science develops by convergence. The naive view thus fails. Moreover, the failure of the naive view highlights a key problem for epistemic views of scientific progress: how do we square justification and warrant with convergence?

An alternative to the naive view attempts to reconcile convergence with justification, and find a way to treat an agreement as justified even when there is no shared justification. One route is to say that an agreement is warranted when each party to the agreement is justified. This allows that justifications are not shared and so admits the possibility that agreement by convergence is warranted. From this conception of warranted agreement, it presumably follows that an agreement (about something true) is knowledge if each party to the agreement justifiably believes the topic of agreement. Let's call the view presently outlined *differentially justified community knowledge*, or *differential knowledge*, for short:

> The agreement of a community is knowledge if every member of the community knows the topic of agreement, and an agreement is warranted if every member is justified, even if members don't share justification.

Differential knowledge makes sense, in a way, of the community being justified, but it does not allow us to articulate the community's justification. In the individual case, we may (often) say what an individual's justification is: when an individual is justified we may ask what her process of believing is and what distinguishes her process from processes that do not produce justification; we may ask, for example, "with what evidence does she support her belief?" However, because there's no uniform process of believing that creates convergence agreement, it seems impossible to articulate what the justification of the community is; we cannot ask "what is the evidence that supports the community's agreement?" since there is no evidence that the community agrees about. This is a break in the symmetry of ordinary, individual knowledge and differential knowledge. Advocates of an epistemic conception of progress may find differential knowledge uncomfortable for that reason. However, their choices are limited. On the one hand, we cannot look to consensus to articulate a justification because there's little consensus. On the other hand, we cannot look to convergence to articulate a justification because convergence doesn't give a clear picture of a process leading to agreement.

Because of this, I think that differential knowledge gives us a way of talking about agreements as knowledge, but it does not clarify the notion that the agreement is knowledge: there's no special *analogy* here, only a way of speaking.

Differential knowledge confronts an immediate difficulty in leaving out the social and communal contribution to scientific development. In chapter 2, I argued that scientific development is the result of convergence rather than consensus, and that convergence is more profitable form of scientific development than consensus. Convergence contributes to the accuracy of agreement, but does not do so by entering into the reasoning of scientists. As a consequence, an important feature of scientific agreement—convergence—is something over-and-above the reasoning of individual scientists. Indeed, convergence is inessential to scientific representations satisfying differential knowledge. This means that an important explanation of scientific reliability lies in facts ignored by differential knowledge.

This is problematic for differential knowledge because the sole locus of assessment for differential knowledge is activity of individual scientists. Convergence itself is outside the scope of differential knowledge, since at most differential knowledge considers only features that have to do with whether individuals know. Since convergence is not a factor in any individual reasoning, differential knowledge does not include the contribution of convergence in scientific development. Consequently, differential knowledge describes scientific development incompletely.

The epistemic conception of progress is not only incomplete, it is otiose: adding knowledge to an otherwise complete description of scientific development adds nothing. Suppose one posses an extensive description of an episode of scientific development, and that the description encompasses non-epistemic factors as well as epistemic ones such as reliability and rationality (both at the individual and communal levels) without identifying any of these elements with knowledge or warrant. Presumably, on an epistemic conception of scientific progress, adding a further identification of knowledge within this development will improve our description of the episode. I don't think that it does.

Scientific development is a complex phenomenon. Our antecedent concepts will guide our ultimate theoretical picture of science, but that does not mean that they will have a role in the ultimate picture we produce. An analogy due to Richard Boyd [Boy80] clarifies this thought.[8] Consider the question 'are long chain polymers molecules?' If this question were posed to a chemist, she would proceed to describe the various features of long chain polymers, comparing and contrasting those features with typical molecules. This is all the chemical story there is to tell about long chain polymers. It answers the question, but not by answering 'yes' or 'no'. There is a complex structural story to tell about long chain polymers, but further description in terms of molecules adds nothing over and above this story. (Of course, we could resolve the question by stipulation and announce that long chain polymers are molecules. Since we could equally correctly announce that they are *not* molecules, it is clear that a decision one way or the other adds nothing to the original story.) The concept of molecules is otiose in long chain polymer descriptions.

Likewise, the concept of knowledge is otiose in the description of science. Scientific development is a complex process involving individual and communal phenomena, and rational and reliable processes; some of the important processes aren't representation generating, and the notions of rationality and reliability are, therefore, not applicable. These factors hang together in complex ways. Given a description of these (and other) phenomena, we have said what there is to say about a scientific development. We

---

[8]Boyd's discussion in [Boy80] was influential in the production of many of the thoughts contained in the present chapter, but, whereas he and I differ in several respects regarding scientific development, especially regarding consensus, it is difficult to develop the thoughts of the present chapter in ways that make my own ideas natural extensions of his. Boyd's position is that the distinction between justifying and non-justifying processes is not one that a theory of knowledge should make because the dialectical nature of science means that scientific methods are evolving. As a consequence, Boyd takes it that formerly justifying processes cease to be justifying because improvements to method raise the bar. However, Boyd's position seems to equate justification and method.

could identify elements of this development with knowledge, or stipulate that the end product is knowledge. However, as is the case with long chain polymers, we could just as easily decline to do so without loss in our description of scientific development. The epistemic conception of progress wants to ask, "But is science knowledge?" Well, there are complex stories to tell about scientific developments, and that development merits interest over and above asking whether a topic of scientific agreement is accurate. So there is a question "what differentiates typical scientific agreement about a truth from mere agreement about it?" that is an analog of "what differentiates knowledge from mere true belief?" However, once we've told the story about the difference, saying whether that difference makes the agreement knowledge adds nothing to the story.

Epistemic conceptions of scientific progress are thus incomplete, this is a important objection to epistemic conceptions. Nevertheless, advocates of an epistemic conception may supplement the conception with appropriate further concepts to recifiy the incompleteness. If, with these revisions in hand, they can show that knowledge is still *the central* concept for understanding scientific progress, epistemic conceptions of progress survive.[9] However, because convergence is an important feature of scientific agreement, knowledge cannot remain a central concept in understanding scientific development; features of scientific development are better understood without appeal to knowledge. Thus, I turn to arguments that knowledge cannot be given a central role; the principle reason will be that knowledge obfuscates important features of scientific development.

Knowledge is ambiguous between reliable processes of believing truly and rational processes of believing truly. Looking at this ambiguity in the concept of knowledge helps us see how the concept of knowledge obfuscates features of scientific development. Let me offer the following provisional definitions: a reliable process of believing is one that would not typically produce (or maintain) the beliefs that it does unless

---

[9]Advocates of an epistemic conception of progress would still need to handle the objection that knowledge is otiose to development of science.

they were true; a rational process is one that follows norms of cognition. The history of philosophy is full of examples in which processes are merely one or the other of these sorts. For example, many skeptical arguments that turn on the possibility of error are designed to show that no matter how careful we are to reason according to norms, there is a chance that we go wrong and, hence, that rationality is unreliable. Conversely, arguments against induction appear to be arguments that it would never be rational to accept induction because any argument on its behalf begs the question; this puts the reliability of induction in question only via our rational expectations—even if induction were reliable, according to those arguments, it would still not be rational.

The history of science witnesses separation of reliable and rational belief formation processes. Consider Earnest Rutherford's famous 1909 gold foil experiment. In that experiment, Rutherford passed alpha particles (helium nuclei) through a thin sheet of gold foil onto a detecting screen. Rutherford observed that a tiny fraction of the particles in the beam scattered across the detecting screen far from the main beam. Rutherford compared the angles of deflection of these particles with predictions from his model of the atom, with which he developed precise accounts of the interaction of an alpha particle with the positively charged nucleus of gold atoms. Rutherford's model was widely held to show that atoms of gold (and atoms more generally) had a central positive charge whose magnitude was sufficient to measurably affect alpha particles by creating the variety of scatter he observed; this magnitude was found to be in proportion to the atomic number of gold.

It is arguable that this conclusion was a rational one. This point is rather subtle because there was no stable "solar system" model of the atom. Nevertheless, it could not have been reliable because the interactions of subatomic particles with atomic nuclei are not typically captured with classical electrodynamics. Of course, Rutherford's calculations were entirely classical. As such, the process by which Rutherford arrived at his conclusion was not one that typically would produce correct predictions.

An objection arises to this discussion of rationality and reliability in Rutherford's experiment: my provisional definition of the two notions is too slippery to make any forceful point. Rutherford's calculations agreed with experiment, but the solar system model wasn't stable. For all I have said, we could go either way on the rationality of conclusions based on his calculations. We need a precise account of rationality before we can say more. Likewise for reliability: Rutherford's experiment was reliable for his particular purposes and the particular variables he was predicting; but the strategy isn't reliable for sub-atomic interactions generally. My provisional definitions of rationality and reliability, so the objection goes, are too vague to allow us to draw any particular conclusions about the subject in question—my discussion shows nothing at all.

To the contrary, my discussion shows exactly that knowledge is ill-suited to the task at hand and obfuscates the developmental process we seek to describe. Attending to refinements in the concept of knowledge (e.g., identifying justification with rationality or with reliability) does not show that one or the other is the *right* way to think about knowledge, but that there are multiple interesting investigations to be made. In looking at Rutherford's experiment, we see decisions and experimental procedures that were important to the development of science. Rather than looking at those decisions strictly in terms of knowledge, we may ask both about the reliability of the processes they involved and their rationality. Experimental investigations admit a similar treatment, and there are several ways to consider the reliability of the experiments as well as their reliability as inputs to decision making. The slipperiness of the notions of rationality shows not that we need to refine a concept of rationality, but that the subtle phenomena under investigation, rather than fitting one refined and best conception of rationality, should be described in terms suitable to the facts of which they are a part. Profitable description of scientific activity arises not from conceptual refinement, but from conceptual proliferation. To get our descriptions right, we need not only more careful concepts, but more of them—and knowledge is but one (ambiguous) concept. Knowledge, therefore, cannot be the central concept for understanding scientific development.

The value of conceptual proliferation is especially important as we consider ways in which science is a social phenomenon. As we move to the social level, concepts of knowledge, which are principally directed at individual belief formation, are less clearly applicable. Consider, for example, a hypothetical scientist whose goal is to produce an influential scientific result, and to be recognized as the first to do so: which research she pursues and how she pursues it will depend on factors about the community in question. [10] Attempting to understand such scientific activity in terms of processes of believing (i.e., the processes to which justification applies) while ignoring the complex social factors such as trust, authority, and practical urgency cannot do justice to the scientific development involved. These social factors are highly influential in scientific discovery, and matters of discovery are inseparable from certification. Hence, the focus on concepts for individual belief formation obfuscates developmental processses central to science.

The epistemic conception of progress requires that we privilege concepts of knowledge and justification in describing scientific development. Science is progressive exactly if it develops in a certain sort of way. Collateral features of development are at best irrelevant. Consequently, we may focus either on reliability or on rationality to the detriment of our understanding regarding the other factor. Recall that the epistemic conception of progress requires some principle like differential knowledge to connect knowing with the product of science. Such a principle requires that we view scientists in terms of how they know topics of scientific agreement. Rather than investigating scientists' activity in terms of the goals which direct their behavior, the epistemic conception of progress conceives their activity in other terms: such an approach surely obscures the scientist whose goal is to explain, predict, or control.

---

[10] See Kitcher [Kit93, ch. 8.3] for a discussion of how a hypothetical scientist might rationally decide about such cases.

It might be argued that knowing is a prerequisite to success in explanation (or prediction, or control) but it nevertheless obscures the activity of explaining to focus upon the knowledge involved when the task is not knowing. (Success in each of these activities seems to me to turn more on accuracy of representations than knowledge; that is, one can succeed without knowing because lack of warrant does not preclude success.)

Contemporary debates in epistemology have often focused on the distinction between reliable processes of believing and rational processes of believing in an effort to determine which is really knowledge. The present discussion shows that such a distinction is helpful to understanding scientific development, but a discovery of which is knowledge is not. Each of the refinements to a concept of knowledge that we might employ may be useful in thinking about different aspects of scientific research. Moreover, few aspects of scientific research may be completely understood by focusing strictly on these epistemic concepts.

There is a final point to be made about cognitive diversity and knowledge. I have argued that scientific communities include individuals who disagree about scientific methods. These disagreements have been exemplified in previous chapters. Many of these cases involve scientists who disagree about whether some proposed bit of evidence is sufficient basis to accept some representation as accurate. I have argued that the scientific community is better when such disagreement is allowed, and that agreements among individuals who thus disagree are better than consensus agreements. Allow, for a moment, that at most one scientist can be right when there are disagreements about whether some bit of evidence is sufficient reason for belief. I contend that a such a disagreement is a disagreement about justification. But, if such disagreements are profitable for the scientific community, then it is better that some scientists are unjustified in their beliefs. The epistemic conception should surely rule against belief that is unjustified, but that is the sort of belief (along with justified belief) that produces the best sort of scientific community. Consequently, the epistemic conception of progress fails.

Some might try to rescue the epistemic conception by claiming that while unjustified beliefs promote progress toward knowledge, their elimination is nevertheless progress. Just as inaccurate beliefs may promote progress toward accuracy, unjustified beliefs may promote progress toward knowledge. But this misses the point: science does not eliminate methodological disagreements, while it does eliminate inaccuracies. Accuracy does emerge from scientific activity, while methodological agreement does not. Moreover, the methodological uniformity that epistemic conceptions offer as an ideal would be a poor state of the scientific community.

5.3 Knowledge and Progress

Alexander Bird argues for the epistemic conception of progress by asking us to imagine a hypothetical scenario in which a scientific community forms its beliefs by some "very weak or even irrational" method [Bir07b, 66]. However, despite the infirmity of their method, the community's beliefs are true, but they never receive any confirmation apart from their weak method. Then, at some later turning point, a member of the community comes to know that the community's method is weak, and persuades them that the method is "unreliable." The scientific community then rejects their old beliefs because they realize the weakness of the method that was their basis. The community then begins acquiring true beliefs on the basis of a justifying method that makes those beliefs knowledge.[11]

Bird says that according to a semantic approach, we have progress that begins early in the episode, followed by a sudden regress at the turning point, and then progress again. According to the epistemic approach, there is no progress until the turning point. Bird contends that the turning point is when "intuitively" progress

---

[11]Bird's verbal description of the episode does not actually contain this description of finally acquiring true beliefs; however, his depiction of it, which is just like figure 5.1 depicts this occurring, so I include it here.

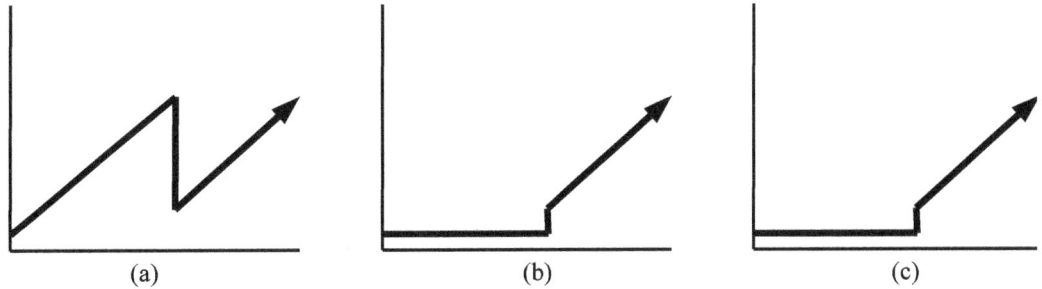

FIGURE 5.1. These diagrams depict changes in (a) truth , (b) knowledge, and (c) what Bird alleges is "intuitively progress" in his thought experiment. This diagram replicates one in [Bir07b]

begins. The three descriptions are depicted in figure 5.1.

Because development regarding truth and progress don't match, Bird concludes progress isn't semantic. Furthermore, because development regarding knowledge and progress do match, he thinks we have reason to believe that progress is epistemic.

This argument presents two challenges to the view of this dissertation. First, it purports to show that semantic changes aren't progress by providing a counterexample, and, second, it purports to establish the epistemic nature of progress by generalizing from the fit of the epistemic conception and "intuitive" progress in his particular case.

One difference between Bird and me on progress is a matter of our goals. An interest of progress seems to derive from two sources. First, progress is invoked in evaluations of scientific change. We want to understand when and whether science improves. Second, progress is invoked in response to an objection to a variety of scientific realism. Realist philosophers of science propose that science achieves truth. Such views are subject to an objection that we know that our current science is the site of some errors, and scientific development does not occur by strict accumulation of truth, i.e., scientific development does not involve a series of discoveries that become permanent parts of scientific lore. This particular objection to strict accumulation realism is effective regardless of whether realism is formulated in terms of knowledge or truth; since truth is a necessary condition for knowledge, strict accumulation of knowledge occurs only if strict accumulation of truth does as well.

Realists respond to this objection that truth is a kind of ideal that we can expect science to approximate in successively truer theories. Realists sophisticate their thesis by claiming that science exhibits a developmental pattern of *improving* with respect to the standards they propose. (Consider a realist response to the considerations of chapter 3: oxygen exists and behaves in many chemical interactions in the way that chemistry says that it does. Realists might offer this as an element of contemporary science that is error free, meeting the realist standard without qualification.) The slogan that realists have attached to this sophisticated version of realism is "science progresses toward truth."

Thus understood, the meaning of 'progress' is less a matter of the antecedent joints in a concept and more a matter of the theoretical role it must play. 'Progress' becomes a kind of place holder for whatever developmental story is told to recover scientific realism from its objectionable, naive ancestor. From this standpoint, the concept of progress begins with a question, "what variety of development does science exhibit?" Given an answer, we may ask "What vestiges of the strict accumulation realist story are preserved?"

This sets up strict accumulation realism as a dialectical starting point for realist philosophy of science. But the substantial question is what it even means to "preserve" the strict accumulation story. There are as many varieties of realism as there are theories of justification and semantics for scientific hypotheses. Presently, we must at least find motivation for distinguishing between the epistemic and semantic conceptions of progress as they manifest a revision of naive scientific realism.

The explanatory defense of realism is the motivation for scientific realism. Consequently, the principled motivation for distinguishing among the epistemic and semantic accounts of progress is which delivers a better explanation of scientific success.

But the epistemic conception of scientific progress does not produce a superior explanation of scientific success. In order for the epistemic conception of progress to produce a superior explanation of success, justifying processes of believing need to be central to scientific development. But, as I have already argued, they are not. First, among the varieties of processes that are candidates for a precise account of justification, each seems to advance our understanding of particular scientific developments; no one of the refinements is privileged, so justification cannot be privileged. Second, justification is a concept for individual believing processes, but part of understanding is advanced by looking to the social level, justification cannot be central. All the explanatory power either the semantic or epistemic conceptions possess is possessed by the semantic conception, and it does not blur scientific development as the epistemic conception does. If either of these succeeds within the realist's explanatory defense, the semantic one does.

What goes wrong with Bird's thought experiment? The answer is simple: conceptual analysis can't tell us anything about contingent matters of scientific development. From the perspective on scientific realism according to which it is an explanatory theory, such contingent matters are what's at issue in scientific progress.

The view of science presented in this chapter, and in this dissertation in general, may be found at odds with a certain naturalistic attitude toward science. According to that naturalism, scientific reasons for belief are *the* reasons to accept science. But the present view does not take such reasons seriously because it denies that reasons are the cause of scientific agreement.

However, this objection misunderstands my view. The reasons of individual scientists are important to the generation of scientific agreement, for without their reasons, individual scientists would not agree. A refinement of the present objection points out that I cannot take scientists' reasons as my reasons for belief because I cite factors, such as convergence, outside scientists' reasoning as important contributors to scientific accuracy.

This version of the objection does not misunderstand my view: I claim we have positive reason to accept topics of scientific agreement. I find that reason in the process by which scientific agreement is reached. Scientists' reasons are involved in that process, but I don't claim to accept the topics of agreement for the reason that scientists do. That's because there is no shared reason for scientific belief. However, to the extent that my view is at odds with traditional naturalism, it is so because traditional naturalism conceives scientific development in a specific sort of way. My view does not espouse the traditional contrary of naturalism, a first philosophy whose goal is to justify scientific practice on extra-scientific, philosophical grounds. I identify scientific process with features that make scientific agreement issue in accurate (or increasingly accurate) representations. I differ from traditional naturalism in denying that individual reasoning exhausts the relevant scientific processes.

REFERENCES

[Bir07a] Alexander Bird. Justified judging. *Philosophy and Phenomenological Research*, 74:81–110, 2007.

[Bir07b] Alexander Bird. What is scientific progress? *Noûs*, 41:64–89, 2007.

[Bir10] Alexander Bird. The epistemology of science—a bird's eye view. *Synthese*, forthcoming 2010.

[Boy80] Richard N. Boyd. Scientific realism and naturalistic epistemology. *Proceedings of the Philosophy of Science Association*, 2:613–662, 1980.

[Boy84] Richard N. Boyd. The current status of scientific realism. In Jarrett Leplin, editor, *Scientific Realism*, pages 41–82. University of California Press, 1984.

[CC98] Martin Curd and J. A. Cover, editors. *Philosophy of Science: The Central Issues*. W. W. Norton, 1998.

[Cha03] Hasok Chang. Preservative realism and its discontents: Caloric revisited. *Philosophy of Science*, 70:902–912, 2003.

[Cha04] Hasok Chang. *Inventing Temperature*. Oxford University Press, 2004.

[DBB76] H. Degn, I. Balslev, and R. Brook, editors. *Measurement of Oxygen*. Elsevier Scientific Publishing Company, 1976. Proceedings of an interdisciplinary symposium held at Odense University Denmark, 26–27 September 1974.

[Fal07] Don Fallis. Collective epistemic goals. *Social Epistemology*, 21:267–280, 2007.

[Fin91] Arthur Fine. Piecemeal realism. *Philosophical Studies*, 61:76–96, 1991.

[Fox71] Robert Fox. *The Caloric Theory of Gases from Lavoisier to Regnault*. Oxford: Clarendon Press, 1971.

[Gie85] Ronald N. Giere. Constructive realism. In Paul M. Churchland and Clifford A. Hooker, editors, *Images of Science*, pages 75–98. Univ. of Chicago Press, 1985.

[Gie88] Ronald N. Giere. *Explaining Science: a cognitive approach*. Univ. of Chicago Press, 1988.

[Gie04] Ronald N. Giere. How models are used to represent reality. *Philosophy of Science*, 71:742–752, 2004.

[Hac82] Ian Hacking. Experimentation and scientific realism. In Jarrett Leplin, editor, *Scientific Realism*, pages 154–172. University of California Press, 1982.

[Hac83] Ian Hacking. *Representing and Intervening*. Cambridge University Press, 1983.

[HP04] Lu Hong and Scott Page. Groups of diverse problem solvers can outperform groups of high-ability problem solvers. *Proceedings of the National Academy of Sciences*, 101:16385–16389, 2004.

[HR82] Clyde L. Hardin and Alexander Rosenberg. In defense of convergent realism. *Philosophy of Science*, 49:604–615, 1982.

[Kit90] Phillip Kitcher. The division of cognitive labor. *The Journal of Philosophy*, 87:5–22, 1990.

[Kit93] Phillip Kitcher. *The Advancement of Science: Science without Legend, Objectivity without Illusion*. Oxford University Press, 1993.

[Kuh70] Thomas S. Kuhn. *Structure of Scientific Revolutions*. University of Chicago Press, 1970.

[Kuh77] Thomas S. Kuhn. Objectivity, value judgment and theory choice. In *The Essential Tension: Selected Studies in Scientific Tradition and Change*, pages 320–39. University of Chicago Press, 1977. Reprinted in [CC98]; page references herein are to that reprinting.

[Lan02] Marc Lange. Baseball, pessimistic inductions and the turnover fallacy. *Analysis*, 62:281–85, 2002.

[Lau81] Larry Laudan. A confutation of convergent realism. *Philosophy of Science*, 48:19–49, 1981.

[Lau84] Larry Laudan. *Science and Values: The Aims of Science and Their Role in Scientific Debate*. University of California Press, 1984.

[Lep84] Jarret Leplin. Truth and scientific progress. In Jarret Leplin, editor, *Scientific Realism*, pages 193–217. University of California Press, 1984.

[Lep97] Jarret Leplin. *A Novel Defense of Scientific Realism*. Oxford University Press, 1997.

[Lew01] Peter Lewis. Why the pessimistic induction is a fallacy. *Synthese*, 129:371–380, 2001.

[Lil48] S. Lilley. Attitudes to the nature of heat about the beginning of the nineteenth century. *Archives Internationales d'Historie des Sciences*, 1(4):631–39, 1948.

[Lin92] David C. Lindberg. *The Beginnings of Western Science*. University of Chicago Press, 1992.

[LL89] Rachel Laudan and Larry Laudan. Dominance and the disunity of method: Solving the problems of innovation and consensus. *Philosophy of Science*, 56(2):221–237, 1989.

[Max62] Grover Maxwell. The ontological status of theoretical entities. In H. Feigl and G. Maxwell, editors, *Scientific Explanation, Space and Time*, volume 3 of *Minnesota Studies in the Philosophy of Science*, pages 3–27. University of Minnesota Press, 1962.

[McM91] Ernan McMullan. Comment: Selective anti-realism. *Philosophical Studies*, 61:97–108, 1991.

[Men61] E. Mendoza. A sketch for a history of early thermodynamics. *Physics Today*, 14(2):32–42, Feb. 1961.

[Mer42] Robert K. Merton. The normative structure of science. In Norman W. Storer, editor, *The Sociology of Science*, pages 267–278. University of Chicago Press, 1942.

[Mer57] Robert K. Merton. Priorities in scientific discovery. In Norman W. Storer, editor, *The Sociology of Science*, pages 286–324. University of Chicago Press, 1957.

[Mus76] Alan Musgrave. Why did oxygen supplant phlogiston? research programmes in the chemical revolution. In Collin Howson, editor, *Method and Appraisal in the Physical Sciences*, pages 181–209. Cambridge University Press, 1976.

[Mus85] Alan Musgrave. Realism versus constructive empiricism. In Paul M. Churchland and Clifford A. Hooker, editors, *Images of Science*, pages 197–221. University of Chicago Press, 1985.

[Nii84] Ilkaa Niiniluoto. *Is Science Progressive?* D. Reidel Publishing Company, 1984.

[PC99] John L. Pollock and Joseph Cruz. *Contemporary Theories of Knowledge*. Rowman & Littlefield, second edition, 1999.

[Pry01] James Pryor. Highlights from recent epistemology. *British Journal for Philosophy of Science*, 52:95–124, 2001.

[Psi99] Stathis Psillos. *Scientific Realism: How Science Tracks Truth*. Routledge, 1999.

[Res94] David B. Resnik. Hacking's experimental realism. *Canadian Journal of Philosophy*, 24:395–412, 1994.

[Saa05] Juha Saatsi. Pessimistic induction and two fallacies. *Philosophy of Science*, 72:1088–1098, 2005.

[Sol01] Miriam Solomon. *Social Empiricism*. MIT Press, 2001.

[Sta06] P. Kyle Stanford. *Exceeding Our Grasp: Science, History and the Problem of Unconceived Alternatives*. Oxford University Press, 2006.

[Ste90] John A. Stewart. *Drifting Continents & Colliding Paradigms*. University of Indiana Press, 1990.

[Ste08] Edward G. Steward. *Quantum Mechanics: Its Early Development and the Road to Entanglement*. Imperial College Press, 2008.

[van80] Bas van Fraassen. *The Scientific Image*. Oxford: Clarendon Press, 1980.

[van08] Bas van Fraassen. *Scientific Representation*. Oxford: Clarendon Press, 2008.

[Whi09] John Whitfield. Nascence man. *Nature*, 21 May 2009.

[Wil00] Timmothy Williamson. *Knowledge and Its Limits*. Oxford University Press, 2000.

[WM09] Michael Weisberg and Ryan Muldoon. Epistemic landscapes and the division of cognitive labor. *Philosophy of Science*, 76(2):225–252, 2009.

[Wor89] John Worrall. Structural realism: The best of both worlds? *Dialectica*, 43:99–124, 1989.

www.ingramcontent.com/pod-product-compliance
Lightning Source LLC
Chambersburg PA
CBHW081419160426
42813CB00087B/2613